The Decline of Service in the Regulated Industries

The Decline of Service in the Regulated Industries

Andrew S. Carron
Paul W. MacAvoy

American Enterprise Institute for Public Policy Research
Washington and London

Andrew S. Carron is a research associate in the Economic Studies Program at the Brookings Institution. Paul W. MacAvoy is Milton Steinbach Professor of Organization and Management and Economics at Yale University and an adjunct scholar of the American Enterprise Institute.

Library of Congress Cataloging in Publication Data

Carron, Andrew S
   The decline of service in the regulated industries.

   (AEI studies ; 306)
   1. Public utilities—United States—Rate of return. 2. Trade-regulation—United States. 3. Independent regulatory commissions—United States. I. MacAvoy, Paul W., joint author. II. Title. III. Series: American Enterprise Institute for Public Policy Research. AEI studies ; 306.
HD2766.C29   338.4'7363'0973   80–26081
ISBN 0–8447–3417–9

AEI Studies 306

Printed in the United States of America

Contents

List of Tables

List of Figures

Preface

The quality of service from the regulated utility or transportation company has not often been a matter of great concern to the consumer. Service has been widely available and accessible on demand, except in natural gas and certain rail freight markets. In the last few years, however, it has become a matter of widespread attention: Service is not what it used to be, nor will it long be as good as it is now.

This analysis probes the causes and consequences of public policies relating to the quality of service in regulated industries. Previous studies have attempted to evaluate service and pricing in one or another of these industries. Here we compile, update, and extend these studies to provide a comprehensive explanation for the decline of service quality. Based on a systematic economic analysis of the process by which service offerings are determined, we project that there will be further declines unless public policies responsible for the present condition are substantially changed in the next few years.

These findings and predictions are based upon ongoing work as part of the Research Program on Government-Business Relations at the Yale School of Organization and Management. The program, which is funded by the General Electric Foundation, the JM Foundation, the Walker Foundation, the Gulf Foundation, the Pfizer Educational Fund, and the IBM Corporation, undertakes systematic evaluations of regulation and other public sector activities as they affect the private sector of the economy. The support provided by these sources is gratefully acknowledged. The sustained assistance of Curtis Spraitzar, Craig Stewart, and Eric Mankin of the research staff at Yale is sincerely appreciated. The critical reviews of the draft manuscript by Marvin Kosters of the American Enterprise Institute, by Robert Crandall of the Brookings Institution, and by Theodore

Keeler of the University of California were essential in developing this published version. James C. Miller III provided many valuable suggestions for content and presentation in the manuscript draft of this book. We are grateful for all of this assistance, and we look forward to further help from our readers in developing a greater understanding of the processes that determine service quality.

1

Service Quality and Regulation

Regulated utilities and transportation companies set the pace for industrial growth and performance in the 1950s and early 1960s. No other sector of the national economy provided services more widely or of higher quality than theirs. Electric and telephone companies advertised their own dependability and promoted the low monthly charges available to residential customers. Natural gas distributors promised the cheapest, cleanest, and most reliable home heating and cooking equipment. The airlines were rapidly enhancing the speed, comfort, convenience, and safety of the most popular mode of intercity passenger transportation. All of these companies also stressed the assurance of fixed rates and expanding service offerings to meet the needs of both old and new customers. By the start of the 1970s, however, the regulated sector was clearly in trouble: rates were up, the quality of service was deteriorating, and availability was restricted in most of the public utility and transportation industries. Rather than extolling more and cheaper service, corporate pronouncements more often apologized for delays and shortages, and urged the consumer to conserve.

Why the reversal in a single decade? Explanations vary with the interests involved. Consumer groups blame the regulated companies for laxness in controlling operating expenses, for mistakes in selecting and adopting new technologies, and for a predilection to pass on to customers the costs of those mistakes. In reply, the companies do point to conditions affecting the economy as a whole, such as increased inflation and reduced productivity growth, but principally they blame their declining performance on the failures of regulation. Indeed, both consumers and producers have criticized the regulators for imposing controls that are time consuming, costly, and —if not unnecessary—at least excessive. The agencies maintain that their legislative mandates constrain them to follow procedures that cause these sluggish and unintentionally perverse responses to changing economic conditions.

Since the regulated public utility and transportation industries play a vital role in providing the infrastructure for productive activities throughout the national economy, it is important to determine the extent and the causes of declines in service. The pervasive attempts to affix blame suggest the existence of a villain with wanton or selfish motives. In our judgment, however, the answer is found in the intricate web of public and private sector activities that shape the performance of the regulated sector. This study describes the deterioration of service quality and economic performance in the regulated industries since the mid-1960s, the causes of those changes, and the means of improvement. The aim of the study is to provide the analytical framework for changes in policy that will lead these industries to restore reliable and efficient service.

Public policy toward this sector has already begun the process of change, spurred by consumer and industry dissatisfaction. As part of regulatory reform, Congress and a few state commissions have moved to address some of the problems. Whether recent reforms will reverse the decline in service quality remains an open question. This study, however, concludes that service in these industries is affected markedly by agency controls and remains a concern. Thus, the content of regulatory reform is a central issue.

The Role of Service Quality in Regulation

Ever since state control over railroads began in the 1860s, the regulatory agencies have directly addressed the service quality issue. Legislatures charged the regulators with the responsibility of guaranteeing service at reasonable prices, particularly for individuals and households otherwise prey to discriminatory or arbitrary offerings by a public utility. While not attempting to deal with all complaints about service for a particular flight, shipment, or repair call, the agencies have attempted to prevent discrimination against individuals within a given class of consumers. Beyond such questions of "fairness," the agencies have dealt with the important strategic issues of service quality in general, across classes of customers, and even across industries.

Regulation is responsible for the level of service quality for at least three reasons. These may be loosely classified as social, economic, and political. No factor by itself can account for the results observed. Rather, it will be seen that these forces combined to create

2

a regulatory system that worked well enough in times of prosperity, but which was incapable of adjusting to reduced economy-wide growth and higher inflation.

The first, or "social," reason derives from the goals of regulation as set by legislation. The commissions controlling prices and service in the railroad, trucking, and airline industries and in the provision of electricity, natural gas, and telephones were instructed to operate in ways beneficial to consumers.[1] Prices should be set reasonably low, in keeping with the cost of service, and that service should be widely available to consumers. At the time of enactment, the new regulatory statute did not fail to promise lower prices, more quantity, and higher quality of service. Early in the development of the regulatory process, the agencies, following the dictates of their legislatures, began to demand wider service of the companies under their jurisdiction. Railroads and public utilities were required to extend their facilities "even if the return on the cost of complying with the order be conceded to be inadequate," as long as the ability of the company to render service was not impaired.[2]

Regulation was pushed further, however, in requiring improved

---

[1] English common law dating from the fourteenth century required all businesses serving the public to accommodate all applicants at reasonable prices. These rules were later carried over to the United States. By the middle of the nineteenth century, the requirement to serve had been abandoned by neglect or omission for most industries. It was recognized, however, that natural monopoly conditions occurred in two important sectors—common carriers and innkeepers—and their duty to serve was retained. Even so, the common law remedy was cumbersome and rarely used. Commissions were then established in a number of states to act as agents for the public. Some of the common carriers challenged these early state commissions. In a landmark decision, the Supreme Court gave states the right to regulate certain businesses (*Munn v. Illinois*, 94 U.S. 113, 161, 24 L.Ed. 77 [1877]): "Property does become clothed with a public interest when used in a manner to make it of public consequence, and affect the community at large." The requirements on common carriers were then imposed at the federal level in the Act to Regulate Commerce (1887) and later legislation covering other industries. As time passed, the interstate transportation and communications industries were often perceived to generate external benefits—the value of the system to existing users increased as new customers were added. As regulation matured, the requirement to serve the public was taken to mean *all* the public (*Wolff Packing Co.* v. *Court of Industrial Relations*, 262 U.S. 522, 535–538, 43 S.Ct. 630, 67 L.Ed. 1103, 27 A.L.R. 1280 [1923]): "[T]he authority of a public grant of privileges . . . imposes the affirmative duty of rendering a public service demanded by any member of the public. Such are the railroads, other common carriers and public utilities." See also Alfred E. Kahn, *The Economics of Regulation: Principles and Institutions. Volume I: Principles* (New York: John Wiley & Sons, Inc., 1970), pp. 21–25.

[2] *Woodhaven Gas Light Company* v. *Public Service Commission*, 269 U.S. 244, 46 S.Ct. 83, 70 L.Ed. 255 (1925), as quoted in W. K. Jones, *Cases and Materials on Regulated Industries* (Brooklyn: Foundation Press, 1967), p. 381. See also The Natural Gas Act, 52 Stat. 824, Section 7(a) (1938), as quoted in Jones, p. 384: "[T]he Commission . . . may by order direct a natural-gas company to extend or improve its transportation facilities . . . if the Commission finds that no undue burden will be placed on such natural gas company thereby."

service for particular classes of consumers. Rural and low-income users were often the intended beneficiaries, although the goal may have been characterized as assuring the provision of "basic" or "essential" services. The reasons for such favoritism included the advancement of economic development through lower-priced or better quality public utility services and, at times, the necessity of obtaining the support of a particular consumer group for the passage of the regulating legislation. More service to rural households, to small communities, and to industries favored for development had become the norm in the 1950s and 1960s.

Once the regulatory process began to favor specific groups, then both rate structure and service offerings had to put burdens on other buyers, the firm's shareholders, or both. Conceivably, the regulated firm might have had to offer some services at rates that did not even cover incremental costs.[3] The less profitable services had to be offset by higher returns elsewhere—their costs could not for long be shifted to the firm's stockholders without imperiling the company's existence. Over the long run, one set of users could be subsidized only if the regulatory authorities imposed higher prices on other consumers. As a result, a number of pricing schemes were established that became embedded in the rate structures of the regulated industries, particularly "value of service" and "cross-subsidy" pricing. In effect, this kind of regulation taxed certain classes of users to provide revenues for extending service to other classes of users.[4]

A second factor in the regulation of service quality may be termed "economic," in that rate controls cannot be administered effectively without some agency surveillance of service offerings. Given the maximum rates permitted by the regulatory commission, the company could increase profit margins by reducing the quality of service, and so its cost. Higher service quality, after all, is costly to the firm and valuable to the consumer. Whether measured in terms of reliability, availability, or some other attribute, to increase

[3] A distinction is made here between costs that, in the short run, are fixed and those that are variable (incremental). The company will not willingly undertake to provide a service for which the additional revenues fail to cover the incremental costs. At times, the firm may choose to sell services at rates that cover incremental costs but contribute little or nothing to the coverage of fixed costs. Yet, while regulators considered it to be in the public interest to provide service to certain classes of users at preferential rates, they were mindful of statutes proscribing "undue or unreasonable preferences or advantages." Civil Aeronautics Act, 49 U.S.C.A., Section 402(c).

[4] Richard A. Posner, "Taxation by Regulation," *Bell Journal of Economics and Management Science*, vol. 2, no. 1 (Spring 1971), pp. 23–29. Short of cross-subsidization, the case decision process used by the regulatory agencies was itself a factor in determining service quality. When making rate requests, companies that could demonstrate their success in extending service to new users were more successful in obtaining revenue increases than other companies.

the quality of a service is akin to providing "more" in a world of scarcity.[5] Thus, the commission must monitor quality of service to control rates effectively: Service quality is not to be reduced during the time between the firm's appearances before the agency; further, a proposal to improve or extend service may be sufficient grounds for a rate increase. Either way, the commission must deal with service quality as part of the price-setting process.[6]

The third, or "political," factor requiring the regulatory agencies to concern themselves with service quality can be found in the administrative procedures built up under regulation. While Congress and the state legislatures intended to establish impersonal, mechanical systems to control excessive prices and profitability in regulated companies, the commissions in practice confront problems of evidence and due process, as well as of interpreting the intent of their enabling statutes. The effect of established administrative procedures and political coalitions has been to create a system that favors preexisting patterns of prices and quantities and that adjusts only very slowly. Agency decisions on entry, prices, and service offerings are often based on historical practice and legal precedent. Current economic conditions and proposals for technical improvements in agency practice are only imperfectly reflected in regulatory actions. These decisions have cost and revenue implications for the companies, which in turn affect service.

Any one of these three factors could have involved the agencies deeply in the quality of services provided by the public utility and transportation industries. But the agencies have gone further and indeed have influenced service offerings and quality beyond the range of legislative mandates, beyond what was needed for effective price control, and beyond what may be explained by administrative friction. The influence has been substantial and in large part responsible for the reductions in service quality of the last several years.

[5] Indexes of service quality for the industries of interest here are developed and explained in chapter 2.

[6] Indeed, two distinguished analysts question whether, given service quality variations, regulation can ever be effective. George J. Stigler and Claire Friedland, "What Can Regulators Regulate? The Case of Electricity," *Journal of Law and Economics*, vol. 5 (October 1962), pp. 11–12: "The ineffectiveness of regulation lies in the regulatory body [being] incapable of forcing the utility to operate at a specified combination of output, price, and cost. . . . [T]he utility can reduce costs . . . by reducing one or more dimensions of the services which are really part of its output: peak load capacity, constancy of current, promptness of repairs, speed of installation of service. . . . Since a regulatory body cannot effectively control the daily detail of business operations, it cannot deal with variables whose effect is of the same order of magnitude in their effects on profits as the variables upon which it does have some influence."

5

To establish this thesis, we shall first describe the regulatory process and show how it affects company price and output decisions. We then consider the effects of regulation on five industries—the electric, natural gas, telephone, airline, and railroad companies—from 1958 to the present.[7] We shall show the direction and magnitudes of the changes in service quality, and the extent to which the stated objectives of the agencies were achieved. During the first third of this period, from 1958 to 1965, economic conditions and regulations produced one set of results; during the 1965–1979 period, however, markedly different economic and regulatory conditions generated quite contrasting results. Each period will be discussed in detail in a separate chapter, to be followed by a concluding chapter on prospects and problems in regulatory reform.

The Regulatory Process

Although each regulatory agency has a unique approach to particular problems, and despite differences across statute mandates and industries, the commissions have shared certain practices. Through rule making and case-by-case review, the agencies approve or disapprove company applications for service and price changes. The firm in turn selects the production methods and determines its own capacity to supply consumers in its designated market regions.

Similarities exist not only in what regulatory agencies control, but also in the decision processes used. Initially, the agency issues a "certificate" to the company selected to provide service across regions, to different classifications of consumers, and for particular

[7] Industries closely related to these (air freight, rail passenger, oil pipeline, intercity bus, urban transport) were omitted because they are substantially less important to the economy. Other major industries have recently been brought under regulation; for example, controls on crude and refined oil products have had some of the same immediate effects, but the controls have not been imposed for a long enough time to establish long-term trends.

Although regulated as to price and entry by the Interstate Commerce Commission, the motor freight transportation industry has also been excluded from this analysis. This is because trucking regulation is different in both technology and regulatory process. Profits are regulated as a percentage of sales rather than as a percentage of the capital stock. Trucking is not a capital-intensive industry; since few fixed facilities are specific to the firm, the trucking companies can adjust the quantity of their services to the profit opportunities. The motor freight industry thus has not been subject to the wide swings in productivity growth that have characterized the other regulated industries, and its modest capital requirements suggest that supply shortages are not a serious concern.

Regulation of broadcasting and financial markets have also been excluded for reasons of differences in process. The justification for regulation in these sectors, which embody only limited aspects of economic regulation of prices, is more social and political.

time periods. Commissions have, for example, established the number of gas, electric, and telephone companies to serve a region; designated classes of industrial, as contrasted with residential, consumers; and set service standards for peak demands as well as for seasonal consumption. Similarly, certification of surface freight carriers has determined the number of railroads hauling goods between two cities, by type of good carried and service offered.

The most important agency controls have been those that set price levels.[8] The first step has usually been to certify a tariff submitted to establish prices or "rates" on scheduled service. As a second step, rather than investigating the rates in thousands of rate schedules in any one company, the regulatory commissions have indirectly but effectively controlled prices by accepting or rejecting company requests for general revenue increases.[9] The agencies approve requests when sufficient evidence is presented to document legitimate cost increases, justified by increased operating costs or by higher depreciation allowances and capital returns required by bond and stockholders. The agency responds to the requests by reviewing studies indicating the nature and extent of these cost and profit increases. In these reviews, the central issue has been whether companies were earning profits sufficient to attract investors and thereby to maintain current and prospective inflows of the capital necessary to maintain and expand service. The proposed increases in profits are measured against the "fair" rate of return on the capital "rate base." In deciding on fair return, agencies have employed measures of the rate base that included the previous capital outlays for plant and equipment used in regulated operations, calculated according to their original costs less depreciation. The agencies have set the fair rate of return within a range established by the testimony of experts. Witnesses for the company and for other interested parties present evidence on what the company should earn to compete successfully for the funds required to replace and, if necessary, to expand capacity. Since these funds must be obtained from prospective debt and equity holders, the determination revolves around what companies have to pay in interest, dividends, and (implicitly) stock price appreciation to maintain the desired level of investor outlays.

The regulatory agencies have focused their attention on profit

[8] Controls on market entry and exit are also important, of course. They are always found in conjunction with price regulations, however, so the effects of nonprice economic regulations can be incorporated into those attributable to price controls.
[9] The request for increased overall revenues of course results in hundreds of individual rate increases, which are changed by means of revised individual service tariffs submitted to the agency at a later date.

rates because they have been the most important factor in allowed revenue increases, as well as the most difficult to evaluate. Historical operating costs and depreciation can be estimated with reasonable accuracy from accounting data, and changes in these costs over time can be detected in a fairly straightforward manner. But levels of "required" profits and changes in these levels have had to be estimated with less methodological rigor and with a much greater degree of subjectivity. In seeking the particular rate of return that the company must have to compete successfully for funds, without unduly burdening customers with higher prices, the agencies have had to resort to judgment. They have reviewed data on recent company disbursements to bond and stockholders, although these data by themselves have not been sufficient to estimate competitive costs of capital. (The costs of equity capital cannot be found directly from recent ratios of dividends to stock prices alone, because investors' expectations of the future rate of growth of dividends affects the current level of stock prices.) Within the range of data, the agencies have set the fair level of returns by choosing among the opinions and forecasts of conflicting experts in case proceedings. This difficult and subjective component of the determination has accounted for one-quarter or more of total revenues in many companies' requests.

With prolonged case proceedings, partly because of abundant expert testimony on the profitability issue, and with rapidly changing economic conditions, the decisions often erred in their findings on the realized and required levels of returns. During the late 1960s and the 1970s, in particular, the process resulted in downward-biased estimates of required revenue increases. This was partly an inherent result of administrative practice. Under conditions of rising inflation, the conventional process would underestimate the replacement cost of capital and the required nominal rate of return. The downward bias increased after the regulatory proceedings were widened to allow substantial access to agency review by those that would be directly affected by revenue increases. These intervenors— representatives of consumer groups, or industrial or commercial buyers of regulated services—presented data and testimony that favored too-low estimates of increased capital costs. They carried weight in the proceedings, regardless of the quality of their estimates, and the process of "splitting differences" resulted in inadequate returns and prices.

The regulated firms responded with a deluge of additional requests for revenue increases. Because of the greater frequency of rate proceedings, the agencies attempted to deal with these requests through larger and more comprehensive investigations. Given the

magnitude of the requested increases, these investigations necessarily placed more weight on the intervenors' case for low prices,
without commensurate consideration for the sufficiency of profit
returns. In an effort to accommodate the interests of all parties and
to stanch the flood of litigation on both sides, the commissions
permitted some increases but held average returns two or three
points below the rates of return on comparable alternative investments of bond and stockholders.[10]

The importance of the political factor was apparent in the New
York regulatory experience. During the late 1960s and early 1970s,
the electric power companies requested increases whenever their
rates of return on investment fell substantially below those of previous years. They went further, however, by requesting additional
revenues when the growth rate of earnings per share declined or
when interest coverage fell (that is, when after-tax income as a proportion of interest was reduced). The companies also entered larger
revenue requests after the commission had permitted larger increases
to other firms. But the New York case decisions also demonstrate
that, in determining the permissible rate of return, the commission
downgraded the amount of the company's request, particularly in
the presence of intervenors and when costs were rising rapidly.[11]

Although not all state and federal agencies followed this particular practice of the New York commission, most considered and
weighted these price-stabilizing factors. On the whole, they allowed
increases in revenues to take account of rising energy costs; further
increases, however, fell short of capital cost changes for long periods
of time during the late 1960s and the 1970s. Only when requests
were made by most of the regulated companies, for good cause and
at the same time so that the case load was "stacked," did the regulatory agencies tend to approve higher rates of return. The commissions, besieged by requests and by contention as costs went up,
moved too little and too late.

Regulatory Effects on Service Quality

These price controls had second-round effects on service offerings.
This can be demonstrated by considering two scenarios. In the first,

[10] Testimony of Virginia A. Dwyer, before the Federal Communications Commission
regarding American Telephone and Telegraph Company's petition for determination
of fair rate of return (March 8, 1979), pp. 4–6.
[11] Paul L. Joskow, "Pricing Decisions of Regulated Firms: A Behavioral Approach,"
Bell Journal of Economics and Management Science, vol. 4 (Autumn 1973), pp. 118–40; and
Paul L. Joskow, "The Determination of the Allowed Rate of Return in a Formal
Regulatory Hearing," *Bell Journal of Economics and Management Science*, vol. 3 (Autumn
1972), pp. 632–44.

the economy is growing rapidly with low inflation rates. Materials, energy, and capital cost increases are small and productivity growth rapid, so that more regulated industry service can be provided without the firm's having to seek a rate increase. On the demand side, real income growth brings with it increased requirements for utility and transportation services, which encourage the companies to invest in new capacity. This expansion permits economies of scale to be realized and, combined with the low rates of inflation and improved technology, serves to reduce the unit costs of providing service. With constant rates and falling unit costs, therefore, the companies generate higher profit margins on larger volumes of service. The improved profit opportunities are an added inducement to new investment, which in turn improves the quantity and quality of service and spurs further productivity gains. The process is then repeated, as the availability of improved service at lower prices triggers growth in demand for the services of these industries exceeding that for the rest of the economy. Regulation has only a marginal effect on the industry's operations, since most of the fixed agency constraints fail to bind because of the superior performance of the regulated industries, as shown in a stylized manner in figure 1.

The second scenario unfolds during periods of high inflation and low demand growth. As prices fall behind costs, the regulated companies are denied rate relief to such an extent that in the long run their revenues would not be sufficient to provide for equipment replacement and capacity expansion. They cannot maintain production to meet current demands or expand production to meet new consumers' future demands. These results occur in steps as shown in figure 2. Slower economic growth reduces rates of capacity utilization, thereby increasing the fixed-cost burden per unit of output and choking off new investment, reducing the rate at which productivity improvements are realized. Inflation of prices for the plant, equipment, and material used in producing these services further raises unit costs. The companies then go to the commissions seeking rate increases, but those granted are inadequate. Without a sufficient increase in revenues, the regulated company realizes lower profit margins and net receipts fall. This in turn leads to dividend cuts, reducing the capital market value of the firm's securities, thereby raising the dividend required per dollar of new capital additions.[12]

[12] As inflation rates were increasing during the period under discussion, dividend and market price "reductions" should be viewed in real rather than nominal terms. Although nominal dividends were actually cut in some instances, often the attrition in values took place through the failure of regulated firms' dividends to keep pace with the rise in inflation rates and market returns.

FIGURE 1
REGULATORY EFFECTS IN A GROWING ECONOMY WITH LOW INFLATION

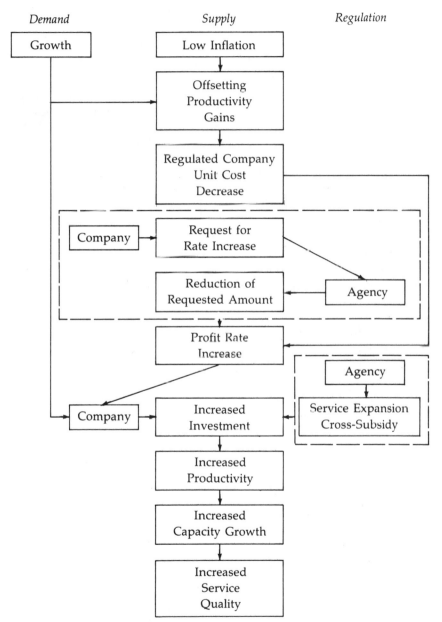

NOTE: Economic growth and low rates of inflation insulate investment and productivity from the effects of agency actions.

FIGURE 2
Regulatory Effects under Recession and Inflation

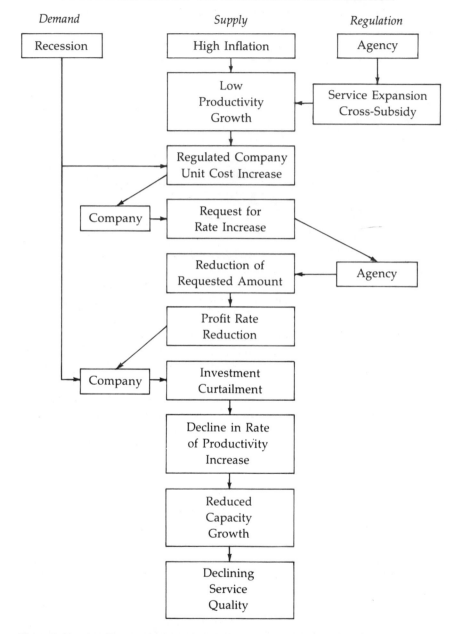

NOTE: Lack of sufficient productivity gains to offset cost increases. Costs are passed through, triggering request for rate increase.

The regulated company then has to reduce both internally and externally financed capital outlays; without these outlays, the capacity to continue to service current and prospective customers is reduced. Just as the regulatory process amplifies the effect of a healthy economy on regulated firms in the first scenario, so inflation and recession are more acutely felt in the regulated industries than elsewhere in the second scenario.

These steps constitute the responses of service quality to regulation. Of course, at any point the process can be reversed if there is an alternative response—if the regulatory agency accepts a sufficiently large request for a revenue increase so that rates of return are increased, or if the company develops new technology to reduce costs and negate the urgency of the request.

In fact, the second scenario dominated the late 1960s and early 1970s, and such alternative events did not occur in the late 1970s, when costs were increasing and regulatory agencies were preoccupied with the political effects of rate increases in periods of high inflation. What did happen after the late 1960s was that inflation-induced cost increases triggered the sequence shown in figure 2. Regulatory agencies granted insufficient revenue increases relative to the level of service required, causing investment and then productivity declines and stimulating additional requests for rate increases. Because the regulatory agencies continued to delay and to reduce firms' requests, sequential reductions took place in investment and service growth and, in the end, service quality declined. These events complicated the job of the regulators by perpetuating consumers' negative attitudes toward these industries. Basically, however, this price-profit-investment-service "nexus" was the logical result of the prevailing economic and regulatory conditions. It determined the declining service performance of the regulated companies from the late 1960s through the entire 1970s.

It might be argued that the higher levels of service quality prevailing in the 1960s were excessive, and that the increased stringency of rate control has now returned these industries to a more socially desirable quality level. At issue is the appropriate level of service. Optimal service quality may be simply defined as that level for which the additional willingness to pay (marginal revenue) falls short of the marginal costs of providing the service. Market failures, however, may prevent the price mechanism from operating to produce the desired level of quality, just as they would affect the determination of optimal quantities. In the case of regulated industries, natural monopoly conditions have forced the interposition of the regulatory commissions, which weakens the price mechanism. Moreover, the presence of externalities suggests that the level of demand registered by individual income considerations will be inadequate.

To measure the extent of market failure that justifies regulatory intervention in favor of higher service quality would be an impossible task given the current state of knowledge. In succeeding chapters, however, specific actions by regulators will be noted. Such activities, when placed in the context of the existing political system, indicate a willingness to enhance service quality—at least for the benefit of particular interest groups. Further, the findings of excess service quality in the literature are few. One might expect to encounter more studies like that of Douglas and Miller, but even they found higher service quality to be confined to a few markets with excessively wide price-cost margins (where service dissipates the excess profits).[13] Thus, it is suggested that the declines of service quality in the 1970s are moving the industries away from—not toward—the optimal level. The higher quality of service in the 1960s was closer to optimal, to the extent that regulation was effective in holding down excess profitability and supplementing offerings to correct various market failures.

[13] George W. Douglas and James C. Miller III, *Economic Regulation of Domestic Air Transport* (Washington, D.C.: Brookings Institution, 1974), pp. 68–75.

2

The Growth of Service Quality, 1958–1965

In the late 1950s, the economy entered a period of sustained growth and low inflation. Real gross national product (GNP), which had increased at a 2.1 percent annual rate during 1952–1958, grew at 3.6 percent annually from 1958 to 1961, and then 5.2 percent a year until 1965. The inflation rate did not exceed 2 percent through most of the 1952–1965 period. Interest rates on three-month Treasury Bills rose only gradually from 2 percent in the early 1950s to 3 percent in the early 1960s.[1] This performance set high standards for subsequent economic conditions, and indeed it turned out to be twice the growth rate and no more than one-third the inflation rate experienced over any sustained period in the late 1960s and the 1970s.

The regulated industries participated in and contributed to the good health of the economy at that time. To some extent, this was necessarily the case because the growth in manufacturing and housing required large and sustained increases in service from the public utilities. In addition, rising real incomes created increased demands for energy and telephone services, for business and leisure travel on the airlines, and for surface freight shipments.

A further impetus to growth in the regulated industries came from the supply side. Expanded production induced higher productivity per worker because it meant that improved equipment could be added more rapidly and also that latent economies of scale could be more fully exploited, particularly in the distribution systems

---

[1] *Economic Report of the President* (January 1979), table B–2, "Gross national product in 1972 dollars, 1929–78," p. 184; table B–3, "Implicit price deflator for gross national product, 1929–78," p. 186; and table B–65, "Bond yields and interest rates, 1929–78," p. 258.

TABLE 1

PRODUCTIVITY CHANGE IN THE
REGULATED INDUSTRIES, 1958–1965

(average annual rate of change in output per man-hour, in percent)

Industry	1958–1961	1961–1965
Electric	5.5	5.6
Natural gas	7.0	7.6
Telephone	7.8	5.4
Airline	−0.9	10.7
Railroad	8.3	7.0
Private domestic economy[a]	2.6	4.0

NOTE: Unless otherwise indicated, the industry groupings used in this and subsequent tables are those of the Department of Commerce Standard Industrial Classification (SIC) system: Electric (generation and distribution, SIC 491), Natural gas (distribution, SIC 492), Telephone (SIC 481), Airline (SIC 45), and Railroad (SIC 40). Where shown, "unregulated services" include the following components of SIC 50–90: wholesale and retail trade; insurance agents, brokers, services; hotels and other lodging places; personal services; miscellaneous business services; auto repair, services, garages; miscellaneous repair services; motion pictures; amusement, recreation services; educational services.

[a] Including the regulated industries given above.

SOURCES: U.S. Department of Labor, Bureau of Labor Statistics, Office of Economic Growth, unpublished data (November 1977); *Economic Report of the President* (January

of the electric, telephone, and gas companies.[2] Most of these industries experienced rates of labor productivity increase that exceeded those of the rest of the economy over the 1958–1965 period (see table 1).

The sources of high productivity growth varied from industry to industry. Economies of scale were important in electric power on both plant and distribution system levels. As the size of generating units increased, production costs per kilowatt-hour declined, and as more firms expanded their transmission facilities, industry-wide unit costs decreased. At the same time, the larger plants and the improvements in the technology for pooling capacity across companies enabled the industry to take advantage of "large numbers" prop-

[2] Worker productivity growth was also quite high in rail transportation even though demand for rail services stagnated in this period; but this in part followed from reduced employment.

erties that permit reduced reserves against peak demands.[3] Output per employee-hour thus grew at a fairly steady rate of between 5 and 6 percent a year during this period, although in the 1960s more of this improvement may be attributed to shifts in the capital-labor mix. Similarly, systems growth led to productivity gains in the natural gas and telephone industries. Gas pipeline transmission and retail distribution benefited from increasing returns to more complete utilization of the large pipelines installed in the early and middle 1950s.[4] The telephone companies, by taking advantage of technical improvements in automatic call switching and in microwave transmission of long-distance calls, substantially reduced labor requirements per unit of output. The rapid rate of expansion of phone service in larger communities also increased productivity because the new technologies introduced in the process of capacity expansion had inherent economies of scale.[5]

In contrast, productivity growth in the airlines resulted almost exclusively from the introduction of a new technology—commercial jets—under conditions of rapid demand growth. The transition from propeller aircraft to jets actually reduced productivity in the 1958–1961 period (see table 1); by 1965, however, a full line of jet aircraft, well suited to a variety of missions, was available, and the new technology had achieved widespread use in the industry. Consequently, output per man-hour in 1965 was 50 percent above the level for 1961; the industry's growth rate of 10.7 percent a year was unmatched by any other industry. (Even the airline industry was unable to match this growth rate in later years, since the wide-body aircraft of the 1970s

---

[3] These have been termed "economies of massed reserves." See E. A. G. Robinson, *The Structure of Competitive Industry*, rev. ed. (Chicago: University of Chicago Press, 1958), pp. 26–27. Changes in technology also resulted in more capital-intensive, more fuel-intensive, and hence more productive operations (when measured by output per man-hour); stable real prices for capital inputs and falling real prices for fuel encouraged this form of input substitution. See Stephen G. Breyer and Paul W. MacAvoy, "The Federal Power Commission and the Coordination Problem in the Electrical Power Industry," *Southern California Law Review*, vol. 46, no. 3 (June 1973), pp. 664–70; and W. R. Hughes, "Short-Run Efficiency and the Organization of the Electric Power Industry," *Quarterly Journal of Economics*, vol. 76, no. 4 (November 1962), pp. 592–612.
[4] Economies of scale in gas transmission are a function of the "two-thirds power rule," by which costs increase slightly more than proportionately to diameter but capacity increases by more than the square of diameter. See Paul W. MacAvoy, *Price Formation in Natural Gas Fields* (New Haven: Yale University Press, 1962), pp. 37–41. Until 1965, production increased more rapidly than capacity; thereafter, capacity was added more rapidly than throughput, thereby reducing capacity utilization. Thus, productivity growth slowed in the late 1960s.
[5] Bell Telephone Laboratories, Inc., *Engineering and Operations in the Bell System* (Murray Hill, N.J.: 1977), p. 98.

were less of an improvement than the quantum advance represented by the first jets.)[6]

Three factors accounted for the apparently impressive gains in railroad productivity in the late 1950s and early 1960s. First, the railroads gradually reduced excess employment, causing labor expenditures to fall from 55 percent of total costs in 1955 to 44 percent in 1970.[7] Second, the companies deferred or reduced track and equipment maintenance, which lessened utilization of those types of labor service with the lowest output per man-hour. Finally, they concentrated more heavily on freight operations, which involved greater productivity. These factors had multiplicative effects on productivity, but did not result in more service of the same or higher quality. Indeed, after adjusting for service deterioration and factor shifts, Meyer and Morton concluded that labor productivity in the rail industry probably increased no more rapidly than that in the private domestic economy as a whole.[8]

The lesser performance of railroads aside, productivity gains kept the regulated industries ahead of their wage and capital cost increases. In some cases, productivity growth exceeded factor cost increases so that the public utilities realized reductions in the nominal costs of producing and delivering a unit of service. This implied that prices could be reduced, or at least held constant, while service offerings were increased. The outcome depended on how the regulatory authorities reacted to these new cost advantages and their consequent profit increases.

It should be noted that the productivity indexes presented in this study arguably may be biased by changes in input or output mix. Criticisms have also been leveled against the methodology employed in the Bureau of Labor Statistics data series used here, particularly with regard to the output calculations. Using a different approach, Gollop and Jorgenson have calculated total factor productivity measures for the regulated industries under study.[9] As shown in table 2, their results generally confirm the patterns presented in table 1. Gollop and Jorgenson, however, found rapid pro-

[6] Almarin Phillips, "Air Transportation in the United States," in W. M. Capron, ed., *Technological Change in Regulated Industries* (Washington, D.C.: Brookings Institution, 1971), pp. 124–37; George W. Douglas and James C. Miller III, *Economic Regulation of Domestic Air Transport* (Washington, D.C.: Brookings Institution, 1974), pp. 9ff.
[7] John R. Meyer and Alexander L. Morton, "The U.S. Railroad Industry in the Post–World War II Period: A Profile," *Explorations in Economic Research*, vol. 2, no. 4 (Fall 1975), p. 449.
[8] Ibid.
[9] Frank M. Gollop and Dale Jorgenson, "U.S. Productivity Growth by Industry, 1947–73," Discussion Paper No. 570, Harvard Institute of Economic Research (September 1977).

TABLE 2

Total Factor Productivity in the Regulated Industries, 1957–1966

(average annual rate of change, in percent)

Industry	1957–1960	1960–1966
Electric	3.96	2.07
Natural gas	− 1.46	1.82
Telephone	3.08	2.17
Airline	− 1.14	4.85
Railroad	1.21	4.36
Unregulated services	0.23	1.10
Total U.S. economy	− 0.49	1.19

SOURCE: Frank M. Gollop and Dale Jorgenson, "U.S. Productivity Growth by Industry, 1947–73," Discussion Paper No. 570, Harvard Institute of Economic Research (September 1977).

ductivity growth in the railroads during the early 1960s after a sluggish performance in the late 1950s.

Rate Cases, Regulated Price Levels, and Profits

The energy, transportation, and communications companies experiencing increased consumer demands and high productivity growth faced bright prospects indeed. With constant prices, falling unit costs, and growing markets, revenues and profits should have increased substantially. This could have occurred, however, only if regulation did not require lower prices or more investment for building capacity to extend service. What in fact happened? Were the companies able to increase profitability, or did the regulators force price reduction and service expansion?

The companies made infrequent requests of the regulatory agencies for revenue changes and actually sought fewer increases in the early 1960s than in the late 1950s (see table 3). Between 1958 and 1961, price increases for these industries averaged only half the increases in the price index elsewhere. And commissions' requests for reductions, along with voluntary and profitable reductions, later brought about a slight decline in price levels. After 1961, prices fell slightly in four of the five industries at a time when the economy-wide price level was rising at 1.8 percent a year (see table 4).

The industries had little to gain from requesting an increase,

TABLE 3

Rate Case Proceedings, 1962–1965

Industry	Average Number of New Proceedings — Per year	Average Number of New Proceedings — Percentage change 1959–1961 to 1962–1965	Allowed Revenue Changes per Year (millions of dollars) — Increases	Allowed Revenue Changes per Year (millions of dollars) — Decreases
Electric	63	−14.3	14.3	42.7
Natural gas	64	−16.6	17.5	21.9
Railroad	212	−10.3	n.a.	n.a.
Airline	1	−66.7	12.8	0.0

n.a. = not available.
SOURCES: For electric and natural gas, EBASCO Investor-Owned Utility Rate Decisions, Increases and Decreases Granted and Pending, 1978, State or Local Jurisdiction. For railroads, investigations and suspensions by the Interstate Commerce Commission. Further evidence comes from another set of data: during 1959–1961, the ICC authorized only one general increase in railroad interstate freight rates, which was for 1.5 percent (Ex Parte 223); no such increases were authorized in the 1962–1965 period (ICC, unpublished data, 1977). For airlines, consolidated airline passenger rate proceedings before the Civil Aeronautics Board.

TABLE 4

Price Increases in the Regulated Industries, 1958–1965
(average annual rate of change, in percent)

Industry	1958–1961	1961–1965
Electric	0.7	−0.3
Natural gas	3.9	−0.5
Telephone	1.8	0.6
Airline	3.3	−0.7
Railroad	−1.5	−1.8
Unregulated services	2.1	1.8
Total U.S. economy	1.6	1.8

SOURCES: Implicit price deflators for gross national product, U.S. Department of Labor, Bureau of Labor Statistics, unpublished data (1978); Economic Report of the President (January 1979), table B–3.

TABLE 5

PRICES AND COSTS IN THE REGULATED INDUSTRIES, 1961–1965
(average annual rate of change, in percent)

Industry	Unit Prices	Unit Costs[a]
Electric	−0.3	0.6
Natural gas	−0.5	0.1
Telephone	0.6	1.5
Airline	−0.7	−5.3
Railroad	−1.8	0.5
Total price-regulated	−0.5	0.7
Unregulated services	1.8	1.7
Manufacturing	0.6	−0.1
Total U.S. economy	1.8	0.9

[a] Unit costs (C_i) are calculated from the changes in unit prices (P_i) and sales price-cost margins, according to the following formula:

$$(C_i/C_o) = [(P_i/P_o) (1-S_i/1-S_o)]$$

where S_i is the ratio of net income to gross revenues. The resulting tabulations are then annualized. Calculations for this period and subsequent periods based on a weighted average of input-cost changes yielded results consistent with those reported here. See Paul W. MacAvoy, *The Regulated Industries and the Economy* (New York: W. W. Norton & Co., Inc., 1979), pp. 72, 136–137.
SOURCES: U.S. Department of Labor, Bureau of Labor Statistics, unpublished data (1979); Standard & Poor's Corp., Compustat (1979).

since cost changes could not have supported a case for substantially higher rates. Costs of inputs—labor, plant and equipment, and materials—were rising in line with economy-wide trends. Increases in labor and capital costs were less than the rapid growth of productivity, so the costs of the "value added" to each unit of output were virtually constant over the period. The cost of materials inputs, primarily fuel, rose modestly.[10]

At the same time, service volumes expanded in response to regulation. Average costs on an accounting basis rose somewhat as companies extended service, with regulation holding price levels stable or calling for small reductions (see table 5). This caused price-cost margins to narrow slightly for all but the airline industry, while such margins were increasing in the rest of the economy; the surge in sales volume, however, was more than adequate to maintain returns on invested capital. The regulated industries registered uni-

[10] Airline fuel costs actually fell with the introduction of the fuel-efficient jets, which burn less costly fuel than the gasoline used by earlier piston-engine aircraft.

TABLE 6

PROFITABILITY OF THE REGULATED INDUSTRIES, 1961–1965
(average of annual rates of return on investors' value, in percent)

Industry	Actual Return	Market Equivalent Return[a]	Difference[b]
Electric	5.9	5.1	+0.8
Gas transmission	4.3	7.7	−3.4
Gas utility	5.4	5.6	−0.2
Telephone	2.4	5.3	−2.9
Airline	23.9	3.5	+20.4
Railroad	8.4	5.9	+2.5
Unregulated services	7.4	10.9	−3.5
Market total[c]	8.2	—	—

NOTE: "Rate of return on investors' value" is the market value-weighted average of interest, dividends, and stock price appreciation divided by the market value of all securities for that industry.
[a] Stock market and bond market returns are derived by adjusted industry-specific risk premium (Beta).
[b] Actual return less market equivalent return. A positive difference is a measure of the extent to which investors were overcompensated for the riskiness of the particular investment.
[c] Composite return for approximately 1,400 publicly traded firms. Market equivalent return equals actual return for market total, by definition.
SOURCE: Authors' calculations based on Standard & Poor's Compustat (1978). For a description of the methodology used, see Paul W. MacAvoy, *The Regulated Industries and the Economy* (New York: W. W. Norton & Co., Inc., 1979), appendix D.

formly higher returns on book value at a time when economy-wide returns were falling.[11]

This combination of cost reduction, rate control, and service improvement seems to have resulted in modest rates of return to holders of the regulated companies' debt and equity. The profit experience is shown in table 6, in which both expected and realized rates of return for stockholders are given for the early 1960s. The indication from these estimates is that the companies did not provide in interest, dividends, and stock price appreciation more than what was earned on investments of comparable risk, except in the airlines, where new equipment and expanding demand produced profitability of about four times that found in comparable industries. With less than expected returns in gas and telephone investments bal-

[11] Authors' calculations based on Standard & Poor's Compustat (1979).

ancing the windfall returns in airlines, on the whole a portfolio of investments in regulated companies did no better nor any worse than one containing companies of comparable risk elsewhere in the economy.

Who then gained from increased productivity if the investors did not? The answer has been suggested by the growth in service. During this period, the commissions increasingly required the regulated companies to employ rate structures and to offer services that would promote more rapid expansion of higher-quality service. An implicit agreement was struck between agencies and firms: demand increases and cost reductions were allowed under regulation to yield higher returns on investment. This higher return, however, was not paid out in dividends, but was used instead to generate funds for improved service to final consumers.

The Growth of Service

The regulatory agencies, as a matter of course, imposed bureaucratic service rules on public utility and transportation markets. They also pressured firms to charge uniform rates across new and old services (rate averaging) regardless of cost differences, both to make rates more "just" across classes and to subsidize the higher-cost extensions of service to new customers within a class. Rate averaging, even in the presence of higher production or delivery costs for the incremental services, was intended to encourage the introduction of new service. (More rapid installation could be accomplished on the fringe of established markets if the higher costs of doing so were "averaged in" with the rates charged existing customers.) The quantity of service expanded rapidly. At the same time, service quality improved or held steady at a high level (see table 7).[12]

Electric power shortages were few, and those that did occur

[12] We have developed measures of service quality for the regulated industries in an attempt to capture more of the attributes of these services than are apparent in the data on output quantities. In compiling two indicators for each industry, we have tried to evaluate the service intended to be offered—the data on electric and gas reserves, airline Q.S.I., and boxcar turnaround time—and the realized quality levels. In some cases, these measures approach closely the ideal indicators of quality; in others, the lack of suitable data force the use of less precise or accurate indexes. The index numbers should be analyzed for the direction of change and the level relative to the base year. Less importance should be attached to comparison of magnitudes across industries, given the diversity of the indicators and the resulting indexation. For public utilities, the measure is reliability of service. The most important aspect of service quality for a transportation company is the expected travel time, including frequency delay and stochastic delay; see Douglas and Miller, *Economic Regulation of Domestic Air Transport*, pp. 80–108. These are measured directly for the airlines and are proxied by boxcar turnaround time for the railroads.

TABLE 7
SERVICE QUALITY IN THE REGULATED INDUSTRIES, 1958–1965
(service quality index, 1958 = 100)

Industry/Index[a]	1961	1965
Electric		
Expected capability margin	144	109
Outage rate (1969 = 100)	n.a.	n.a.
Natural gas		
Reserve capacity	90	84
Curtailments	100	100
Telephone		
Dial tone delay	111	140
Trouble reports	93	96
Airline		
Q.S.I.[b] (1961 = 100)	100	137
Load factor	107	109
Railroad		
Loss and damage (1960 = 100)	98	89
Boxcar turnaround time	96	100

n.a. = not available
[a] Higher index indicates improved service.
[b] Q.S.I. = quality of service index.
SOURCES: Service quality indexes are authors' calculations, based on industry and government data, adjusted for comparability.

Electric: Gross reserve margin at peak, excess of actual capacity over demand in marker year predicted at the time of the capacity decision, Edison Electric Institute, *Electric Power Survey* (various years). Electric utility outages and load reductions (except storm related) relative to electricity consumption, Federal Power Commission, quarterly news releases (various years); U.S. Department of Energy, "Statistics of Electric Utilities in the United States" (various issues).

Natural Gas: Ratio of natural gas reserves to annual gross production, American Gas Association, *Gas Facts* (1978). Ratio of natural gas curtailments to annual sales, Federal Power Commission/Federal Energy Regulatory Commission, ad hoc special reports and Form 16 Reports of Gas Supply and Requirements (various years).

Telephone: Percentage of customer-dialed calls encountering dial tone delays exceeding three seconds during busy hour and customer reports per 100 stations, American Telephone and Telegraph (1978).

Airline: Civil Aeronautics Board (CAB) airline Quality of Service Index for three selected interstate routes (frequency, capacity, number of stops), based on *Official Airline Guide* (various issues). Inverse load factor for domestic trunk scheduled service, CAB, *Handbook of Airline Statistics* (1973) and *Supplements* (various years).

Railroad: Freight loss and damage claims as a share of revenues, Association of American Railroads, *Freight Loss and Damage* (various issues). Turnaround time for boxcars (all types) adjusted for changes in average trip length and train speed, based on Interstate Commerce Commission (ICC), Annual Report (various issues); Association of American Railroads, "Operating Statistics, Class I Line-Haul Railroads," and "Operating and Traffic Statistics, Class I Line-Haul Railroads," (various issues); ICC, Bureau of Accounts, "Ratios of Empty to Loaded Freight Car-Miles by Type of Car and Performance Factors for Way, Through and All Trains Combined" (title varies; 1958, 1963, 1969, 1973); ICC, Form OS–A (unpublished data, 1979).

resulted from unexpected weather damage of scattered pieces of equipment rather than from systematic shortages of generating capacity. Telephone dial tone delay was reduced by one-third after 1958, with trouble reports up fractionally. Airline flight frequencies and seat availability improved while flight time itself decreased substantially.[13] Railroad freight loss and damage worsened marginally during the early 1960s, while the turnaround time for boxcars (a measure of the availability of capacity for standard carload service) held steady. Only in the natural gas industry were conditions deteriorating noticeably, as reserved backing for the production and delivery of gas by the interstate pipelines was being reduced; reliability of deliveries of gas, however, was not affected by the reduction of reserve backing during this period so that consumers experienced no immediate losses in quality.

Service quality increased in part because of quite high rates of investment in these industries. Offering better energy and transportation services at peak demand periods required more capacity. Capacity growth in the regulated sector was rapid, generally exceeding that of the manufacturing sector (see table 8). The only exception was investment in new plant by the railroad industry, which, while increasing capacity and service offerings on long-haul bulk transportation, was failing to maintain service on many short-distance and branch lines where trucking had won over the market. Even here, however, the high reported rates of equipment investment for the railroad industry demonstrate the attempt to improve service on the main lines.[14]

As a consequence of lower prices, greater capacity, and improved service, sales of the regulated companies grew rapidly. The growth rate of production in the regulated industries (except for the railroad industry) exceeded that of the general economy by at least two percentage points a year over the 1958–1961 period. During 1961–1965, the production growth rate in all five regulated industries exceeded that of the economy, even though the economy's growth rate had increased by two points over the earlier period. Airline service experienced the most spectacular growth, at 14 percent a

[13] In the case of the airlines, it has been asserted that the resulting level of service quality was excessive. But even here, the intention of the commission was to promote cross-subsidization and the resulting quality was an effect of the competitive environment. See Douglas and Miller, *Economic Regulation of Domestic Air Transport*, pp. 68–75.

[14] The railroad industry was also shifting from ownership to lease of equipment and rolling stock. This shift, along with decreasing service demands, makes it difficult to develop a meaningful analysis of railroad investment performance. Except for transitory seasonal peaks and harsh winters, however, the railroad industry was not faced with capacity shortages.

TABLE 8

INVESTMENT AND CAPACITY GROWTH
IN THE REGULATED INDUSTRIES, 1958–1965
(average annual rate of change, in percent)

Industry	Measure and Source	1958–1961	1961–1965
Electric	Net capital stock (BEA)	5.3	4.1
Gas transmission	Net capital stock (BLS)	4.0	3.1
Telephone	Net capital stock (BEA)	6.7	7.5
Airline	Net capital stock (BLS)	21.1	8.8
Railroad	Net capital stock (BEA)	−1.1	−0.6
	Equipment investment (BLS)	9.7	19.4
Manufacturing	Net capital stock (BEA)	0.3	2.4
Total U.S. economy	Net capital stock (BEA)	2.8	4.2

SOURCES: U.S. Department of Commerce, Bureau of Economic Analysis (BEA); U.S. Department of Labor, Bureau of Labor Statistics (BLS).

TABLE 9

RATES OF OUTPUT GROWTH
IN THE REGULATED INDUSTRIES, 1958–1965
(average annual rate of change, in percent)

Industry	1958–1961	1961–1965
Electric	5.5	7.2
Natural gas	5.8	5.6
Telephone	6.0	7.8
Airline	8.3	14.3
Railroad	0.5	5.7
Unregulated services	2.9	5.1
Total U.S. economy	3.6	5.2

NOTE: Output growth is measured in terms of real gross national product.
SOURCES: U.S. Department of Labor, Bureau of Labor Statistics, unpublished data (1978); Economic Report of the President (January 1979).

year over the first five years of the 1960s. Electric power and telephone industry growth rates were remarkably high as well, exceeding 7 percent during that period (see table 9).

By the mid-1960s, the pattern of service performance had become clearly established. Regulation and industry cost reductions had caused prices for public utility and transportation company services to fall relative to those in the unregulated service industries. Falling relative prices induced increases in per capita consumption of regulated services exceeding those in the rest of the economy. Service offerings expanded to meet these demands, both in quality and quantity, partly because specific regulatory policies encouraged such expansion. This can be seen from the behavior of particular rates and services.

Development of the Rate Structure

The thousands of tariffs that make up "rate structure" were a product of company and regulatory agency activity. The companies had to propose the tariffs to account for the complex differences in distance, volume of purchases, time of day, season, and the specific service in effect. The companies had substantial discretion within the overall limitation on rate of return because of the problems of measuring output and allocating costs in capital-intensive industries that are subject to large peak loads, and that are required to meet all demands and provide service on favorable terms.[15] But the agencies had their share of control over the rate structure; they issued standards for the spread of rates, following guidelines for the differences between classes, and directly set the rates for some services while controlling overall revenues.

A number of different pricing arrangements were pursued, sometimes in sequence as the nature of demands and technologies changed, at other times concurrently. The goals were not always consistent nor the tools precise. Hence, any attempt to classify the realized rate structures into a few pure types will necessarily be

[15] Evaluation of cost allocation issues in the regulated industries presents a number of theoretical and methodological problems. The electric, natural gas, telephone, and (to a far lesser degree) railroad industries exhibit aspects of a natural monopoly market structure. Marginal-cost pricing is efficient but leads to losses at all levels of output because average costs exceed marginal costs for all relevant levels of demand. Possible solutions are average-cost pricing, price discrimination, or external subsidies. Thus, a pricing structure that shows prices diverging from incremental costs may be a response to natural monopoly, an explicit income redistribution scheme, or a combination of the two. A closely related problem is the peak load issue. For industries that must build a large capital plant to handle the maximum demand over a cycle (and in which output cannot be stored), there is the question of how to allocate the fixed costs. At peak utilization, the marginal cost to serve an additional customer includes additional capital stock; during off-peak times, there are only the variable costs. Average-cost pricing, or even a system with higher rates for peak service, may involve smaller price-cost margins for peak users than for off-peak users.

unsatisfactory. It must suffice, therefore, to describe the principal pricing schemes that have been attempted, and to suggest certain implications flowing from these efforts.

An important element of the resulting pattern was "value-of-service" pricing, which implies the charging of higher rates to customers whose price elasticity of demand is low. This scheme permits greater growth in the level of output at compensatory rates for industries with latent economies of scale than would a completely cost-based rate structure, because rates are low on services with highly elastic demands.[16] In theory, a rate is set for each class of users according to the elasticity of that class. Class is usually defined by status (business or personal, large or small) and usage (basic or discretionary).[17] Where costs decline substantially at high levels of company output, rates for users with relatively elastic demands may be reduced if the loss in revenue is more than offset by the lower unit costs of higher levels of output.[18] This extension of value-of-service pricing has been termed "growth subsidization." As a matter of course, the regulated companies actively seek lower rates to expand service where unregulated firms provide competitive services. The companies continue to charge higher rates where there is no direct competition, so profit margins become quite disparate across different classes of service.[19]

In the 1960s, the agencies, mindful of the reasons for regulation, controlled certain rates so as to expand further the scope of regulated services to favored classes of consumers. These activities changed the rate structure in a manner that created rate disparity beyond that found in any strict value-of-service schedule. In contrast to growth subsidization, which strictly increases the firm's profitability on all services, regulated firms began receiving instructions to serve one

[16] See W. J. Baumol and D. F. Bradford, "Optimal Departures from Marginal Cost Pricing," *American Economic Review*, vol. 60 (June 1970).

[17] Proration of fixed costs, however, is typically not part of the equation, and variable costs are assigned to classes as a whole. Within a particular class, some users of some services may at times pay less than the incremental cost of the service, so that there exists some cross-subsidization among members of a class. This aspect of uniform pricing within a class of users, independent of cost differences within the class, is termed "rate averaging," and may exist whether or not the rate for the class as a whole is determined by inverse elasticity pricing rules. See, for example, Southwestern Bell Tel. Co., 95 P.U.R. (n.s.) 1, 4–5 (Arkansas Public Service Commission, 1952), approving a rate policy that "takes the company's properties, revenues and expenses for the state as a geographical and jurisdictional unit, and fixes exchange rates which equitably distribute the charges for telephone service among the users."

[18] See Paul L. Joskow, "Inflation and Environmental Concern: Structural Changes in the Process of Public Utility Regulation," *Journal of Law and Economics*, vol. 17 (October 1974).

[19] In the presence of profit controls, demands on the regulated firms tend to increase; unit costs fall where there are economies of scale, and in some cases overall prices decline to final consumers, as shown in chapter 1.

class of customers at rates that yielded below-average or even negative profits, while another class generated high profits. The gains and losses, in theory, balance to provide the company with the overall rate of return deemed appropriate for the public utility. Thus, the range of rate disparity is extended, while the average rate is not changed. In effect, this scheme, termed cross-subsidization or "internal subsidization," is a form of income redistribution among classes of users and is usually justified on social rather than economic-efficiency grounds.[20]

Practicing value-of-service and cross-subsidization rate control took many forms. Some agencies pressed public utilities serving large geographic areas to charge all subscribers the same monthly rate for service, even though it was more costly to serve more distant subscribers or those with more complex connections to the system. In the transportation industries, commissions set rates according to distance without sufficient regard for the effects of traffic volume on unit costs. This practice made margins too low on some thinly traveled routes and, conversely, too high on well-traveled segments.

The actual extent of cross-subsidization, or subsidization of one service by excess profits on another, varied from one regulated industry to another. By the early 1960s, commissions had agreed with the electric utilities to offer relatively low residential service rates that would encourage customers to install electric heating, cooling, and hot water systems.[21] Gas distribution companies, faced with rising supply prices for natural gas from the interstate pipelines, were widely advised by state public utility commissions to limit residential rate increases but to increase industrial and commercial rates.[22] The telephone companies, regulated by the Federal Communications Commission (FCC) and by state public utility authori-

[20] See G. C. Eads, L. L. Johnson, and W. F. Hederman, Jr., "The Role of Cross Subsidization in Federal Regulation: Preliminary Phase I Report" (Santa Monica: Rand Corp., 1978), pp. 29ff.
[21] For a more complete description of the motivations for cross-subsidization in electric power, see H. Bierman, Jr., and J. E. Hass, "Inflation, Equity, Efficiency and the Regulatory Pricing of Electricity," *Public Policy*, vol. 23, no. 3 (Summer 1975), p. 303; J. P. Blair, "The Politics of Government Pricing: Political Influences on the Rate Structure of Publicly-Owned Electric Utilities," *American Journal of Economics and Sociology*, vol. 35, no. 1 (January 1976); Sam Peltzman, "Pricing in Public and Private Enterprises: Electric Utilities in the United States," *Journal of Law and Economics*, vol. 14 (April 1971), pp. 109–49; and H. W. Pifer and E. L. Scholl, "An Analysis of Recent Electric Utility Rate Increases," Temple, Barker, and Sloane, Inc., the Energy and Environment Group (June 1975).
[22] See A. C. Aman and G. S. Howard, "Natural Gas and Electric Utility Rate Reform: Taxation through Rate-Making?" *Hastings Law Journal*, vol. 28, no. 5 (1977); Paul W. MacAvoy and Roger G. Noll, "Relative Prices on Regulated Transactions in the Natural Gas Pipelines," *Bell Journal of Economics and Management Science*, vol. 4, no. 1 (Spring 1973); and S. Wellisz, "The Public Interest in Gas Industry Rate Structure," *Public Utilities Fortnightly* (July 19, 1962, and August 2, 1962).

ties, developed a "separations" formula for allocating costs of basic residential service between interstate and intrastate use. Over time, the formula agreed upon among the agencies assigned an increasingly larger share of these costs to long-distance calling. In general, long-distance rates were higher than they otherwise would have been, and residential service and installation charges were lower.[23] In fact, residential rates may have been below the direct costs of providing the service (this was certainly true for installation), and may have been the lowest profit margin service overall.[24] The Civil Aeronautics Board (CAB), which ended most direct subsidies to the trunk carriers for local service by the middle 1950s, maintained high rates on long-distance service to compensate for low rates on local service to smaller communities. The CAB suggested this policy because short-haul air transportation was an integral part of the transportation system and therefore had to be subsidized by above-cost fares in other mileage brackets where traffic was not as sensitive to the level of fares.[25] The railroads were also under strong pressure from the Interstate Commerce Commission (ICC) to continue non-remunerative branch line service with the costs covered by higher rates on high-volume bulk service.[26] Even though some industries may have exploited residential customers, the pattern was to favor residential and rural consumers at the expense of industrial or commercial users.

Later in the period, it became even more evident that the rate structure was contrived by the regulatory agencies. As limited price

[23] Report, FCC Docket 20003 (1976), p. 768.

[24] An appraisal of the Illinois Bell Company in 1967 showed that rates set equal to marginal costs would have been double actual levels for local calls and one-sixth of actual toll rates. Also, all rates that year were below those that an unregulated monopoly company would have charged, with the exception of interstate toll business service. This analysis implied that regulation had kept prices on interstate calls at above-cost levels to provide an internal subsidy of local service. See S. C. Littlechild and J. J. Rousseau, "Pricing of a U.S. Telephone Company," *Journal of Public Economics* (1975), pp. 35–36.

[25] R. M. Johnson, Phase 9 Decision, U.S. Civil Aeronautics Board, *Domestic Passenger-Fare Investigation, January 1970 to December 1974* (Washington, D.C., 1976), pp. 862–63.

[26] See Theodore E. Keeler, "Railroad Costs, Returns to Scale, and Excess Capacity," *Review of Economics and Statistics*, vol. 56 (May 1974), pp. 201–8; Ann F. Friedlaender, "The Social Costs of Regulating the Railroads," *American Economic Review*, vol. 61 (May 1971), pp. 226–34; R. Harris, "Economics of Traffic Density in the Rail Freight Industry," *Bell Journal of Economics and Management Science*, vol. 8 (Autumn 1977), pp. 556–64; Richard C. Levin, "Regulation, Barriers to Exit, and Railroad Investment Behavior," unpublished manuscript (1978); Richard C. Levin, "Allocation in Surface Freight Transportation: Does Rate Regulation Matter?" *Bell Journal of Economics and Management Science*, vol. 9, no. 1 (Spring 1978), pp. 18–45; Paul W. MacAvoy and John W. Snow, eds., *Railroad Revitalization and Regulatory Reform* (Washington, D.C.: American Enterprise Institute, 1977); and Michael Conant, *Railroad Mergers and Abandonments* (Berkeley: University of California Press, 1965).

increases became necessary to cover increased costs on some services, commissions responded by allowing increases only for those groups of consumers whose interests were to be least favored by regulation. As shown in table 10, industrial gas rates increased more than rates to residential consumers. Intrastate telephone rates, for service mostly to home consumers, went up less than interstate rates for business usage (as indicated by relative long-distance rates subject to comparable cost increases). Industrial electric rates were reduced while residential rates increased, principally because lower industrial prices permitted realization of economies of scale in bulk industrial services, which serve in turn to moderate costs for other customers. Local service airline fares were an apparent exception. They increased at a relatively more rapid rate for two reasons: their costs went up faster than those of the trunk airlines, and the trunk airlines succeeded in avoiding CAB-required cross-subsidization as much as possible by turning local service over to specialized carriers. Where

TABLE 10

RATE STRUCTURES IN THE REGULATED INDUSTRIES
(1958 = 100)

Industry/Service	1965 Rate Level
Electric	
Small residential	104
Industrial	92
Natural gas (retail sales)	
Residential	107
Industrial	117
Telephone	
Intrastate long distance	91
Interstate long distance	100
Airline	
Domestic trunk fare	106
Local service fare	113

SOURCES: For electric, data on electric bills for three largest private utilities and three largest public (municipal) utilities, Federal Power Commission, *Typical Electric Bills* (various issues). For natural gas, American Gas Association, *Gas Facts* (1977); U.S. Department of Energy, "Sales of Fuel Oil and Kerosene" (1978). For telephone, data from American Telephone and Telegraph (1979). For airlines, Civil Aeronautics Board, *Handbook of Airline Statistics* (1974) and *Supplements* (1976, 1978); CAB, *Commuter Air Carrier Traffic Statistics* (various issues)

31

they were required to maintain local service, the trunk carriers removed most of their equipment, thus neutralizing much of the attempt at cross-subsidy. (Only when the indicated profitable flight frequency fell below the mandated two per day did true cross-subsidy occur.)[27]

In fact, value-of-service and cross-subsidy pricing may or may not have come about as a result of the agencies' sometimes contradictory efforts. The mixed pattern of rate structures was not always successful in effecting the desired pattern of subsidies. A determination depends on the resulting price-cost margin and whether the favored class of consumers had elastic or inelastic demands. The regulatory agencies acquiesced in some of the firms' proposals and imposed requirements of their own on others. Their continued desire to pursue several goals, social and economic, eventually placed heavy demands on the regulatory process and then, inevitably, on the firms themselves. Something had to give—one or more of the agency's goals for service quality, internal subsidization, the profitability of the firm, or some combination of all of these.

Overall, however, policy required the companies to develop patterns of selective rate changes to protect certain constituent groups from higher prices. These groups, principally home consumers and other users of "basic service," on the whole received more and higher-quality service than they would have in the absence of regulation. The regulated "infrastructure" of transportation, energy, and communications services provided rate certainty and service continuity at high levels of quality.

[27] See U.S. Department of Transportation, Regulatory Policy Staff, "Service to Small Communities—The Cross-Subsidy Question," in Paul W. MacAvoy and John W. Snow, eds., *Regulation of Passenger Fares and Competition among the Airlines* (Washington, D.C.: American Enterprise Institute, 1977), pp. 81–154.

3

Regulation and Declining Service Quality in the 1970s

After 1965, an increasingly inhospitable economic climate combined with regulation to produce substantial cost inflation but only modest rate increases for the regulated industries. Just as regulation reinforced the favorable economic conditions of the early 1960s to advance growth and service quality in the public utility and transportation sector, it magnified the adverse effects of unfavorable conditions in the late 1960s and the 1970s. As a result, the high level of service quality wrought by regulation in the earlier period was eroded during the 1970s.[1] Although this has been widely noted, little has been done to explain these losses or to implement policies to reverse them.

Regulatory practice remained unchanged through most of this later period, even though it was no longer consistent with—and often antithetical to—the agencies' goals. Why did they not therefore change the practices or reduce the stringency of regulation? In part, the answer lies in the agencies' continued ability to achieve some of their objectives, particularly those benefiting certain favored groups of customers, thus encouraging those groups to resist any change in the regulatory process. The force of these interests limited the extent of change despite the obvious reduction in total service offerings.

The condition of the regulated industries in the 1970s had its genesis in the late 1960s. The transition during 1965–1969 to inflation and slower growth under stringent rate controls will be described first, to be followed by a detailed review of the performance of the regulated companies and of the resulting quality of service in the 1970s.

[1] Some reduction in service quality, as an alternative to reduced output or higher prices, may have been an appropriate response to the economic conditions of the period. This choice, however, was never explicitly made.

The Regulated Industries in the Late 1960s

By all measures, the national economy did not perform as well after 1965 as it did in the first half of the decade. Real GNP growth fell from an average annual rate of slightly more than 5 percent in 1961–1965 to slightly less than 4 percent in 1965–1969. At the same time, the annual rate of increase in the GNP price deflator more than doubled from 1.8 percent to 3.9 percent. Interest rates, as represented by three-month Treasury Bills, also more than doubled, rising from 2.9 percent in 1960 to 6.7 percent a year in 1969, effectively cutting business investment by one-half and reducing residential investment from a level of net growth to mere replacement of the housing stock.[2] These conditions followed the Johnson administration's deficit financing of extensive domestic and Vietnam war programs; their persistence signaled movement onto a path of lower growth and higher inflation.

This new path had a major effect on behavior in the regulated industries. The slower rate of economy-wide growth led to reduced rates of demand growth for utility and transportation services. Smaller increments of demand required fewer additions to capacity. Thus, it took the regulated industries longer to install new technology and exploit latent scale economies. At the same time, a broadly based slowdown in the discovery and development of important new technologies occurred. As a result, the regulated industries experienced lower rates of productivity growth and, with rising wage rates and capital and fuel costs, unit production costs began to rise rapidly.

With much greater cost inflation at hand, and with the anticipation of reduced rates of demand for previously installed capacity, the companies began to request revenue increases from the regulatory agencies each year rather than once or twice a decade. Faced with more and larger requests, the regulatory agencies acted more frequently, but they failed to approve rate increases large enough to keep up with the cost increases in the five regulated industries. The case decisions kept the average rate increase at a fraction of the price increase for the economy as a whole, and also well below the cost increases actually realized in these industries (see table 11).

The slow and small increases in regulated prices during 1965–1969 in turn reduced operating margins and subsequently the profit rates of public utilities and common carriers. These results were reflected

[2] *Economic Report of the President* (January 1979), table B–2, "Gross national product in 1972 dollars, 1929–78," B–3, "Implicit price deflations for gross national product, 1929–78," and B–65, "Bond yields and interest rates, 1929–78."

TABLE 11

PRICES AND COSTS IN THE REGULATED INDUSTRIES, 1965–1969

(average annual rate of change in percent)

Industry	Unit Prices	Unit Costs[a]
Electric	0.5	2.3
Natural gas	0.1	0.7
Telephone	0.5	1.4
Airline	2.0	4.9
Railroad	1.2	2.5
Total price-regulated	0.7	2.9
Unregulated services	4.5	4.4
Manufacturing	2.5	2.6
Total U.S. economy	3.4	3.0

[a] See table 5.
SOURCES: U.S. Department of Labor, Bureau of Labor Statistics, unpublished data (1979); Standard & Poor's Compustat (1979).

in reduced stock market valuations for the companies (see table 12). Their stockholders earned less than half the market rate of return (except in the gas transmission industry, where economies of fuller utilization of existing plant were still being realized to such an extent that unit transmission costs were not greatly increased; even here, however, returns were below expectations). The improved performance of most regulated industries in the 1969–1973 period was not sufficient to offset the poor returns of 1965–1969; for the eight-year period as a whole, returns adjusted for risk were generally below the market rate (see table 13).

Such were the steps that led to a reorientation of the regulated industries in the 1970s. They occurred to different degrees and with varying rapidity across these industries. The transportation industries experienced the largest reductions in productivity growth and the largest increases in unit costs at the end of the 1960s. The energy utilities (electricity and natural gas) followed suit in the mid-1970s. As will be discussed below, the timing for the telephone industry followed a different pattern. Stockholder valuations of both transportation and utility industries had been lowered by the turn of the decade, leading to discounting of their stock prices so as to provide rates of return comparable to that of the market during the 1970s. The companies in each of these industries did poorly in the market,

TABLE 12

PROFITABILITY OF THE REGULATED INDUSTRIES, 1965–1978
(average of annual rates of return on investors' value, in percent)

Industry	1965–1969			1969–1973			1973–1978		
	Actual return	Market equivalent return[a]	Difference[b]	Actual return	Market equivalent return[a]	Difference[b]	Actual return	Market equivalent return[a]	Difference[b]
Electric	1.1	5.3	−4.2	5.5	5.1	+0.4	8.5	6.2	+2.3
Gas transmission	3.7	5.2	−1.5	6.5	4.5	+2.0	8.2	6.2	+2.0
Gas utility	1.8	5.3	−3.5	5.1	4.9	+0.2	8.7	6.2	+2.5
Telephone	0.4	5.3	−4.9	6.8	5.0	+1.8	8.2	6.2	+2.0
Airline	1.4	5.3	−3.9	1.3	5.3	−4.0	7.1	6.2	+0.9
Railroad	2.2	5.3	−3.1	8.4	4.9	+3.5	5.8	6.2	−0.4
Unregulated services	10.6	5.2	+5.4	2.2	3.7	−1.5	5.7	6.1	−0.4
Market total[c]	5.2	—	—	4.4	—	—	6.1	—	—

NOTE: "Rate of return on investors' value" is the market value-weighted average of interest, dividends, and stock price appreciation divided by the market value of all securities for that industry.

[a] Stock market and bond market returns are derived by adjusted industry-specific risk premium (Beta).

[b] Actual return less market equivalent return. A positive difference is a measure of the extent to which investors were overcompensated for the riskiness of the particular investment.

[c] Composite return for approximately 1,400 publicly traded firms. Market equivalent return equals actual return for market total by definition.

SOURCE: Authors' calculations based on Standard & Poor's Compustat (1978).

TABLE 13

ACTUAL AND PREDICTED RATES OF RETURN ON INVESTORS' VALUE,
1965–1973

(average of annual rates, in percent)

Industry	Actual Return	Predicted Return
Electric	3.3	5.2
Gas transmission	5.1	4.9
Gas utility	3.4	5.1
Telephone	3.6	5.2
Airline	1.4	5.4
Railroad	5.3	5.1
Unregulated services	6.4	4.5
Market total	4.8	—

SOURCE: Authors' calculations based on Standard & Poor's Compustat (1978).

relative to companies in the unregulated industries, as investors saw that inflation, recession, and regulation were working against their profit margins.

The timing and extent of these patterns occurred in the extreme in the telephone industry. A series of actions taken by the Federal Communications Commission in the mid-1960s led to a comprehensive agency review of the Bell System's rate of return.[3] As a result, telephone company stock prices declined in the middle 1960s, even though prices in the stock market as a whole were rising. Attempts were made to compensate for a declining price-earnings ratio by increasing net earnings. These efforts took many forms, including that of not increasing capital outlays in 1966–1967, a time when demand growth in several areas exceeded switching capacity.[4] The resulting capacity shortages caused serious declines in service quality, with service interruptions in major East Coast cities during 1967–1968. By 1969, service throughout the urban regions of the eastern part of the country was beset by delays in dial tone, repairs, installation of new equipment, and long-distance call completion at peak periods, particularly in the Bell System companies. At that point, the Bell System reversed these policies intended to support previous profit rates and to bolster stock prices in favor of its traditional operating priorities, which emphasized investment to main-

[3] AT&T, Docket 16258, 9 FCC 2d, 115–116, 960, 978–979 (1967); *Public Util. Comm'n* v. *United States*, 356 F.2d 236 (9th Cir.), certiorari denied, 385 U.S. 816 (1966).
[4] American Telephone and Telegraph, unpublished data (1980).

tain and expand service. The company then submitted rate requests to finance the projects. Whether these massive new equipment outlays were profitable, or could even be supported by the reduced profit margins of the late 1960s, is problematical. In that sense, the telephone companies provided the first clear case of sustained cutbacks followed by investment and capacity growth in face of reduced profit margins.

From all appearances, the other regulated industries continued to provide high-quality and even improving service during the late 1960s. Behind the appearance of business as usual, however, there were emerging conditions of capital stringency that would create problems similar to those the telephone industry had seen earlier. Reduced reserve margins against future and current demands were already evident in the electric and natural gas industries. With the necessity for curtailing investment, reduced service was awaiting all of the regulated industries in the 1970s.

Inflation, Recession, and Regulation, 1969–1978

The general economic conditions prevailing at the turn of the decade were not favorable to any industry. Production growth rates had declined and inflation had increased, so that "paper" profits grew while taxation reduced real rates of return on investment.[5] This condition held for both unregulated and regulated companies. Even so, few suspected the highly adverse state of affairs to come for the regulated companies in particular.

During 1969–1973, real GNP growth fell by half a percentage point, while the rate of increase in the GNP price deflator went up by more than one percentage point. Over the following five years, real GNP growth fell an additional percentage point, from 3.4 percent in 1969–1973 to 2.3 percent in 1973–1978. The price deflator rose at an average annual rate of 3.9 percent in 1965–1969, at 5.1 percent a year in 1969–1973, and then at 7.5 percent a year in 1973–1978. The combination of continued inflationary expectations and a monetary policy intended to constrain inflation caused interest rates to increase from 5.0 percent over 1965–1969 to 5.7 percent in 1969–1973, and then to 6.4 percent in 1973–1978.[6] Partly because of these higher financing costs, investment growth fell to slightly more than 1 per-

[5] See William D. Nordhaus, "The Falling Share of Profits," *Brookings Papers on Economic Activity* (1:1974), pp. 169–208.
[6] This is the average interest rate on three-month Treasury Bills; see *Economic Report of the President* (January 1979), table B–65.

cent a year over the 1973–1978 period, thereby adding to the slow-down of productivity, capacity, and GNP growth.

The combination of lower GNP growth and higher inflation spread across all sectors of the private economy. Particularly in the regulated industries, however, reduced demand growth slowed down productivity growth, which, with higher factor prices, resulted in substantially greater increases in unit production costs. Lower demand also resulted in the regulated companies' having to spread high capital costs over smaller output growth rates for purposes of setting regulated rate levels. The combination of rising operating costs and rising overhead costs per unit of sales made the case for revenue increases even more urgent.

The greatly reduced productivity of the regulated industries is indicated in table 14. Between the early 1960s and the early 1970s, productivity improvement rates fell by eight percentage points in the airline industry, and by two points in railroad freight service. There was an eight-point loss in the productivity growth rate in the natural gas industry, principally because output was constrained by regulation of the field price of interstate gas supplies, which caused new gas reserves to be shut-in or to be sold in intrastate markets rather than to go to the interstate transmission companies. Productivity growth fell as well in electric power and in the telephone industry, averaging about 4 percent a year in the early 1970s rather than the 5 to 6 percent range of a decade before. As shown in table 15, Gollop and Jorgenson's total factor productivity series again confirms this pattern across regulated industries.

TABLE 14

PRODUCTIVITY CHANGE IN THE REGULATED INDUSTRIES, 1961–1976
(average annual rate of change in output per man-hour, in percent)

Industry	1961–1965	1965–1969	1969–1973	1973–1976
Electric	5.6	4.9	3.9	0.1
Natural gas	7.6	5.3	−0.1	−1.7
Telephone	5.4	5.4	4.8	9.4
Airline	10.7	3.0	2.4	2.0
Railroad	7.0	4.5	5.1	−0.8
Total U.S. economy	4.0	2.2	2.4	0.8

SOURCES: U.S. Department of Labor, Bureau of Labor Statistics, Office of Economic Growth, unpublished data (November 1977); *Economic Report of the President* (January 1979).

TABLE 15

TOTAL FACTOR PRODUCTIVITY IN THE REGULATED INDUSTRIES, 1960–1973

(average annual rate of change, in percent)

Industry	1960–1966	1966–1973
Electric	2.07	−0.35
Natural gas	1.82	0.37
Telephone	2.17	1.21
Airline	4.85	3.45
Railroad	4.36	1.71
Unregulated services	1.10	0.08
Total U.S. economy	1.19	0.43

SOURCE: Frank M. Gollop and Dale Jorgenson, "U.S. Productivity Growth by Industry, 1947–73," Discussion Paper No. 570, Harvard Institute of Economic Research (September 1977).

One cause of this reduction in productivity was the lower rate of utilization of capacity, particularly new capacity, consequent from the economy-wide slowdown of demand growth. The capital-intensive regulated industries, which plan investment far in advance based on demand growth, were not able to adjust rapidly to a lower level of final demand growth. Thus, low present profit rates were accompanied by low demand growth rates that made it difficult to capture economies of greater scale and newer technology.

Each of the regulated industries had specific reasons for reduced productivity performance. In the electric utilities, new technology was not forthcoming at the previous rate, and scale economies of existing technologies were in large part exhausted.[7] As fuel prices increased, labor-intensive technologies were more widely adopted and these by themselves caused lower labor productivity growth.[8]

[7] L. Christensen and W. H. Greene, "Economies of Scale in U.S. Electric Power Generation," *Journal of Political Economy*, vol. 84 (1976), p. 655: "[I]n 1955 there were significant scale economies available to nearly all firms. By 1970, however, the bulk of U.S. electricity generation was by firms operating in the essentially flat area of the average cost curve." Lawrence W. Weiss, "Antitrust in the Electric Power Industry," in Almarin Phillips, ed., *Promoting Competition in Regulated Markets* (Washington, D.C.: Brookings Institution, 1975), p. 147: "The large increase in optimal scale relative to demand in the 1950s and 1960s will turn out to be a one-time change rather than a trend." See also R. A. Nelson and M. E. Wohar, "Total Factor Productivity in the Electric Power Industry: A Disaggregated Approach," mimeographed (Newark: University of Delaware, 1980).

[8] This theme is developed at length in Frank M. Gollop, "The Sources of Growth in the U.S. Electric Power Industry" (paper presented at the Conference on Productivity Measurement in Regulated Industries, University of Wisconsin, 1979).

The imposition of environmental and safety regulations on generating plants reduced productivity growth as well.[9] Productivity declines in natural gas resulted from the depletion of gas reserves committed to the interstate pipelines. Telephone industry demand growth continued at high rates, so that new switching capacity embodying improved large-scale technology could be introduced rapidly once the Bell System resumed accelerated investment. But new regulation of work rules and conditions under federal equal employment opportunity and occupational health and safety policies probably reduced labor productivity growth rates from those of earlier periods.[10] Air passenger service experienced lower productivity growth for similar reasons. The technological improvements in the later 1960s and in the 1970s did not compare with the remarkable gains brought about by substituting the jet for the piston engine. As fuel prices increased, cutbacks in service because of higher flight costs increased the overhead burden and brought about declines in productivity growth rates. The decline in the railroads was attributable to falling demands for rail freight service during the recession of the middle 1970s, and to increased resistance to additional reductions in employment as a consequence of rationalization policies for existing systems.[11] On the whole, different combinations of reduced demand growth, higher factor costs, and a reduced supply of significant new inventions caused productivity growth rates to decline in these industries.

These conditions alone would have caused unit production costs to increase substantially. In addition, however, fuel prices rose so rapidly that they added sharply to the costs of producing retail electricity and natural gas, and somewhat less (because of continuing domestic controls on petroleum prices) to the increases in airline passenger and railroad freight operating costs in the mid-1970s (see table 16). (The second round of sharp fuel price increases, in 1979–1980, affected the airlines relatively more than did the earlier

---

[9] Crandall, corroborating the more general results of Denison, concluded that "a 50 percent increase in pollution control outlays reduces output per employee-hour by 1.2 percent, one-third of their annual average increase." See Robert Crandall, "Pollution Controls and Productivity Growth in Basic Industries" (paper presented at the Conference on Productivity Measurement in Regulated Industries, University of Wisconsin, 1979); and Edward Denison, "Effects of Selected Changes in the Institutional and Human Environment upon Output per Unit of Input," *Survey of Current Business*, vol. 58 (January 1978), pp. 24–44.

[10] See tables 14 and 15.

[11] See generally John R. Meyer and Alexander L. Morton, "The U.S. Railroad Industry in the Post–World War II Period: A Profile," *Explorations in Economic Research*, vol. 2, no. 4 (Fall 1975), pp. 449–501; U.S. Department of Transportation, *A Prospectus for Change in the Freight Railroad Industry* (1978), pp. 39–64.

TABLE 16

Fuel Cost Changes in the Regulated Industries, 1958–1977
(percent)

Industry	1977 Fuel Cost as Share of Price	Weighted Average Annual Change in Fuel Cost				
		1958–1961	1961–1965	1965–1969	1969–1973	1973–1977
Electric	37	0.5	−0.2	3.5	14.6	20.5
Natural gas	40[a]	5.2	1.1	0.1	8.0	32.3
Telephone	n.a.	n.a.	n.a.	n.a.	n.a.	n.a.
Airline	19	1.2	0.5	2.8	6.3	20.1
Railroad	20	0.0	−0.3	1.2	5.2	22.0

n.a. = not available.
[a] Field price as share of retail price.
SOURCES: Data Resources, Inc., Cost Forecasting Service (1978); Edison Electric Institute (1977); American Gas Association (1977); Civil Aeronautics Board (1978).

episode. Electric utilities had been successful in reducing their dependence on oil, which by then was in the process of being decontrolled, and natural gas was following a transition price schedule relatively insensitive to world oil prices.) Only in the telephone industry, where fuel costs were a much smaller share of total factor costs, was there a relatively low rate of unit cost increase.

Substantial increases in production costs justified requests to the regulatory agencies for similarly large increases in revenues (see table 17).[12] The agencies generally responded by granting less than the amounts requested, which could be expected, but also less than the amounts required to maintain investment. Price changes in the regulated industries, which in 1965–1969 lagged behind the rest of the economy, were roughly comparable to those in the unregulated service industries during the 1970s. But the allowed price increases were less than the realized cost changes, especially in those industries that use large amounts of fuel (see table 18).

In natural gas, the restrictive rate policies of the Federal Power Commission had caused supply shortages, which in turn required limiting access of industrial users to pipelines and gas supplies at retail. Even though access was limited, industrial gas prices increased at twice the rate of residential prices. Because the shortages contin-

[12] The numbers of cases were much lower for airlines and railroads, because these industries are regulated on the national level. The larger numbers for the utilities represent the multiplicity of state-by-state determinations.

TABLE 17

RATE CASE PROCEEDINGS, 1966–1978

(average annual number of cases and
net revenue requests granted)

Industry	1966–1969	1970–1973	1974–1978
Electric			
Number of cases	42	78	124
Revenues (millions of dollars)	21	802	2,306
Natural gas			
Number of cases	47	64	73
Revenues (millions of dollars)	31	261	651
Telephone			
Number of cases	6	21	24
Revenues (millions of dollars)	69	654	738
Airline			
Number of cases	1	3	7
Revenues (percent increase)	n.a.	4.1	6.8
Railroad			
Number of cases[a]	1	2	6
Revenues (percent increase)	3.4	6.4	7.9

n.a. = not available.
[a] General increases in interstate freight rates authorized by the Interstate Commerce Commission.
SOURCES: See table 3; and American Telephone and Telegraph (1980).

ued to be imposed on industrial users, even these relatively large price increases do not by themselves effectively indicate the total burden implicit in rationing imposed on that group of consumers. Not only did industrial users pay more for natural gas and receive less of the curtailed supply, but their alternative sources of energy— usually fuel oil—increased in price nearly as much as did natural gas (see table 19).

The telephone companies were required by state and federal regulatory commissions to allocate more of the "common" capital costs to interstate long-distance rates. This preserved the basic residential monthly bill insofar as possible, increasing charges on and profits from commercial and industrial consumers that used long-distance service most intensively.

TABLE 18

PRICES AND COSTS IN THE REGULATED INDUSTRIES, 1969–1978
(average annual rate of change, in percent)

Industry	1969–1973		1973–1978	
	Unit prices	Unit costs[a]	Unit prices	Unit costs[a]
Electric	5.7	8.7	14.3	15.3
Natural gas	7.9	8.9	14.6	16.0
Telephone	2.9	5.4	2.5	2.4
Airline	5.6	6.4	8.7	10.5
Railroad	4.4	4.4	9.7	10.3
Total price-regulated	5.1	6.7	9.3	10.0
Unregulated services	4.6	4.7	8.0	7.8
Manufacturing	4.5	4.7	9.2	8.9
Total U.S. economy	5.2	5.1	7.1	7.3

[a] See table 5.
SOURCES: U.S. Department of Labor, Bureau of Labor Statistics, unpublished data (1979); Standard & Poor's Corp., Compustat (1979).

Airlines were an exception. Operating under the newly installed rate-setting policies that resulted from the Civil Aeronautics Board Domestic Passenger Fare Investigation, they no longer had to cross-subsidize by increasing long-haul relative to short-haul passenger fares. With service by main trunk airlines on local or short-distance routes cut back substantially, few remaining growth subsidy opportunities existed in the 1970s.[13]

The railroads made requests for rate increases almost every year after 1967 as a result of rising costs, and the Interstate Commerce Commission granted sufficient rate changes to keep the rail rate index in line with general price level changes; but more of the rate increases were placed on trainload and long-distance services than on carload or short-distance services (see table 20).

In each industry, proposals to the agencies for revenue increases encountered great resistance even though they were justified by cost

[13] George W. Douglas and James C. Miller III, *Economic Regulation of Domestic Air Transport* (Washington, D.C.: Brookings Institution, 1974), p. 97.

TABLE 19

PRICES AND CONSUMPTION OF
RESIDENTIAL AND INDUSTRIAL FUELS, 1969–1977
(1958 = 100)

	1969	1973	1977
Prices			
Residential gas	107	133	248
Industrial gas (retail)	120	167	567
Industrial gas (direct)	121	189	613
No. 2 fuel oil	119	152	317
Consumption			
Residential gas	171	178	176
Industrial gas	200	205	165

SOURCES: American Gas Association, *Gas Facts* (1977); U.S. Department of Energy, "Sales of Fuel Oil and Kerosene" (1978).

increases. When decisions were made, the allowed increases were concentrated on certain groups of consumers. Generally, industrial consumers paid substantially more than residential consumers and rate increases for the latter were moderated.

With reduced and perhaps even negative profit margins on residential and small commercial sales, incentives to expand and improve the quality of service to these consumers were greatly reduced. This was partly because it was clear that sources to finance growth subsidies could not be found indefinitely. Revenues generated by increased prices on industrial users would not be sufficient in the future to allow for further expansion of service in any and all directions, because of demand elasticity and possible competition from unregulated suppliers in providing new industrial service. Even though the statutory mandate for "common carrier" operations continued, profit opportunities from operating under such mandates were becoming increasingly limited, since both the markets that were the sources for subsidies and those that were their recipients experienced reduced profitability.

At first, the regulated firms were not generally inclined to reduce service offerings. Indeed, investment and capacity additions continued at the high rates of the early 1960s, in spite of reduced profitability (compare the results in table 21 with those in table 8). Because of continuing service obligations, previously ordered capacity coming

TABLE 20

RELATIVE PRICES IN THE
REGULATED INDUSTRIES, 1965–1977
(ratio of industrial to residential prices)

Industry	Terms of Ratio	1965	1969	1973	1977
Electric	Industrial/small residential	0.88	0.90	0.99	1.25
Gas utility	Industrial/residential	1.09	1.12	1.26	2.29
Telephone	Long-distance interstate/intrastate	0.91	0.94	1.00	1.28
Airline	Trunk/local service passenger fare	0.75	0.68	0.64	0.68
Railroad	Carload/less-than-carload ratios of revenues to variable costs	n.a.	n.a.	1.10	1.16

n.a. = not available.

SOURCES: For electric, data on electric bills for three largest private utilities and three largest public (municipal) utilities, Federal Power Commission, *Typical Electric Bills*, various issues. For gas utilities, American Gas Association, *Gas Facts* (1977); U.S. Department of Energy, "Sales of Fuel Oil and Kerosene" (1978). For telephone, American Telephone and Telegraph (1979). For airlines, Civil Aeronautics Board, *Handbook on Airline Statistics* (1974) and *Supplements* (1976, 1978); CAB *Commuter Air Carrier Traffic Statistics* (various issues). For railroads, Interstate Commerce Commission, Burden Study Data, unpublished (1979).

on-line, and perhaps expectations that profits would increase as a result of larger allowed rate increases in the future, the companies moved forward at the earlier investment and capacity growth rates.

Given these rate increase problems, the relative increase in costs over rates caused profit margins on sales to fall again in the first half of the 1970s. With reduced price-cost margins, the transportation companies and public utilities were generally poor investments for stockholders.

During the first phases of the cyclical recovery from the recession of 1974–1975, investments by stockholders in the regulated industries were less profitable than those in other industries, and far less profitable than they were in the late 1950s or early 1960s. Moreover, the riskiness of returns on these investments increased, with added uncertainties concerning the ability of these firms to cover their traditional dividend payments over the new business cycle. In fact, actual returns were low in the early 1970s, from 1.3 percent in the airlines to 5.5 percent in the electric industry and 6.8 percent in the

TABLE 21

INVESTMENT AND CAPACITY GROWTH
IN THE REGULATED INDUSTRIES, 1965–1978
(average annual rate of change, in percent)

Industry	Measure and Source	1965–1969	1969–1973	1973 to Date Given
Electric	Net capital stock (BEA)	5.8	7.0	5.9 (1978)
Gas transmission	Net capital stock (BLS)	4.5	2.8	2.0 (1974)
Telephone	Net capital stock (BEA)	8.4	9.2	6.0 (1978)
Airline	Net capital stock (BLS)	22.4	4.7	−1.8 (1978)
Railroad	Net capital stock (BEA)	0.1	−0.4	−0.2 (1978)
	Equipment investment (BLS)	−2.0	−8.7	n.a.
Manufacturing	Net capital stock (BEA)	5.3	1.8	2.4 (1978)
Total U.S. economy	Net capital stock (BEA)	5.6	3.7	2.7 (1978)

n.a. = not available.
SOURCES: U.S. Department of Commerce, Bureau of Economic Analysis (BEA); U.S. Department of Labor, Bureau of Labor Statistics (BLS).

telephone industry (see table 12). The more depressed gas and railroad investments recovered a little, to the 7 and 8 percent range. Even so, on the whole the regulated companies were realizing returns which were lower than interest returns on less risky bonds.

Without being able to offer an attractive return, the regulated companies continued to go to capital markets for funds. After a point, the amounts both sought and realized fell off. The transportation companies undertook no more than half as much investment in the early 1970s as in the late 1960s. Investment outlays by the natural gas transmission companies were reduced to levels required to maintain deliveries. As a result, the net capital stock in these industries was more or less held at levels achieved a decade earlier. Investment rates in the telephone companies, while still high in

TABLE 22

RATES OF OUTPUT GROWTH
IN THE REGULATED INDUSTRIES, 1965–1977
(average annual rate of change, in percent)

Industry	1965–1969	1969–1973	1973–1977
Electric	7.1	6.3	−0.3
Natural gas	6.5	0.7	−1.6
Telephone	9.2	7.7	7.3
Airline	14.0	3.4	3.9
Railroad	2.4	2.8	−3.4
Unregulated services	4.0	3.9	2.4
Total U.S. economy	3.9	3.4	1.9

NOTE: Output growth is measured in terms of real gross national product.
SOURCES: U.S. Department of Labor, Bureau of Labor Statistics, unpublished data (1978); *Economic Report of the President* (January 1979).

comparison with other regulated industries, nevertheless declined by one-third. The electric companies did not significantly reduce their rates of investment during the late 1960s, but it should be noted that investment was falling increasingly further behind the growth in demand. On the whole, investment was no longer proceeding at a faster rate in the regulated industries than elsewhere in the economy.

The reduction in net investment rates eventually led to reduced rates of production growth. In fact, there was no GNP growth in the electric and natural gas industries by the middle 1970s (see table 22). Airline GNP growth dropped from 14 percent a year in the late 1960s to 4 percent in the middle 1970s, while railroad service growth fell from nearly 8 percent a year to about 3 percent. Of course, these reductions were in keeping with economy-wide recessionary conditions, first in the early and then in the middle 1970s. Before this period, however, the five industries had grown at twice the rate of the economy on the whole, while in the 1973–1977 period the five regulated industries grew at or below the economy-wide rate.[14]

Both regulatory agency and company were concerned about maintaining the quality of service under these conditions. Efforts

[14] Most of the 1.9 percent average annual growth for the regulated sector (table 22) was attributable to the very high rate of growth of the telephone industry—the one industry with sustained investment.

were made in the electric power and telephone industries to adhere to the principle of universal service. To this end, certain policy changes were made, such as adding more to charges for "frills" than for basic service, and imposing on the companies the requirement of providing wider access to basic service for small consumers at lower charges. In the gas industry, existing customers were given rights to service as long as supplies lasted at prices reflecting field supply contracts made in the 1950s. The concept of "essential service" was maintained during the mid-1970s by the Civil Aeronautics Board with the airlines and by the Interstate Commerce Commission with the railroads, as indicated by continued reluctance to allow decommissioning of service.

But even with the regulatory agencies' resistance to service changes, the quality of offerings in these industries declined significantly (see table 23). As can be seen from using the measures described in chapter 2, both electricity and natural gas experienced systematic declines in service quality in the 1970s. Consumers had as much access to electric service as before, but only because peak demands were reduced by the combined effects of fuel price inflation and economy-wide recession. On the whole, available capacity relative to expected demands declined; as shown in table 24, the industry anticipated operating well below the preferred reserve margin of 20 percent during the 1970s.[15] Realized demand did exceed capacity in some regions, and this resulted in a higher rate of power outages.

Customers of gas service did not have as much access in the 1970s as five or ten years earlier. The regulation-induced shortage of field supplies had worked its way through the system to curtailments of industrial and commercial service each year. From 1.3 trillion cubic feet (TCF), or 10 percent of total interstate deliveries in 1972–1973, the shortfalls had grown to 3.6 TCF, or more than 35 percent of interstate deliveries, in the late 1970s (see table 25). The consequent loss of service was highly disruptive in energy markets— buyers with cutoffs went to imported crude and petroleum products supplies, or reduced energy usage and thus final production of goods and services. The interruption system itself degraded service, since it made no allowance for efficiency in final fuel use, or for conservation, or for investment and production in energy-using industries.

---

[15] From the 1950s to the mid-1960s, electric utilities installed new capacity ahead of expected demand. Then, for reasons explained in the text, their ability to expand service became constrained. Serious power shortages in the 1970s were averted only because exogenous factors forced a reduction in demand growth, which offset the supply curtailments.

49

TABLE 23

SERVICE QUALITY IN THE REGULATED INDUSTRIES, 1965–1979

(service quality index, 1958 = 100)

Industry/Index[a]	1965	1969	1973	Latest Year
Electric				
Expected capability margin	109	110	96	62 (1979)
Outage rate (1969 = 100)	n.a.	100	<100[b]	<100[b] (1978)
Natural gas				
Reserve capacity	84	63	52	52 (1977)
Curtailments	100	100	93	76 (1978)
Telephone				
Dial tone delay	140	84	250	329 (1977)
Trouble reports	96	82	82	94 (1977)
Airline				
Q.S.I.[c] (1961 = 100)	137	201	199	163 (1978)
Load factor	109	119	116	106 (1978)
Railroad				
Loss and damage (1960 = 100)	89	73	90	109 (1977)
Boxcar turnaround time	100	90	88	73 (1977)

n.a. = not available.

[a] Higher index indicates improved service.

[b] Electric outage data do not lend themselves to indexation. In 1969, there were no reported load reductions ("brown-outs") and non-weather-related outages were virtually nil. By 1973, load reductions affected approximately 0.1 percent of all power delivered that year, and blackouts had increased tenfold since 1969. Blackouts fell to three times the 1969 level in 1978, while the proportion of power affected by load reductions continued to rise, to 0.5 percent of power delivered.

[c] Q.S.I. = quality of service index.

SOURCES: See table 7.

TABLE 24

CAPABILITY MARGINS IN THE ELECTRIC POWER INDUSTRY, 1958–1979

(percent)

Capability Margin	1958	1961	1965	1969	1973	1979
Expected	18.7	26.9	20.3	20.5	17.9	11.5
Actual	25.9	31.0	22.9	16.6	20.8	36.1

SOURCE: Edison Electric Institute, *Electric Power Survey* (various years).

TABLE 25
NATURAL GAS CURTAILMENTS, 1972–1979

Year (Sept.–Aug.)	Firm (TCF)	Interruptible (TCF)	Percent of Total[a]
1972–1973	1.031	0.285	9.5
1973–1974	1.362	0.218	12.0
1974–1975	2.418	0.276	21.9
1975–1976	2.976	0.444	29.5
1976–1977	3.400	0.449	35.3
1977–1978	3.197	0.416	36.9
1978–1979 (est.)	3.150	0.433	41.7

NOTE: Curtailments of firm services by pipelines are reductions of deliveries from the firm base-period gas entitlements. Curtailments of interruptible customers are based on reductions in normal deliveries to such customers (that is, curtailments over and above normal curtailments of interruptible load). All data exclude curtailments by pipelines of other reporting pipelines.
[a] Total curtailments as percent of total shipments.
SOURCES: For 1972–1973, Federal Power Commission, ad hoc special report. For all other years, abstracts from Federal Energy Regulatory Commission, Form 16 Reports of Gas Supply and Requirements (various years).

During the late 1960s, in an effort to reduce costs and improve earnings, the telephone companies had failed to expand capacity sufficiently to keep up with the rapid economic growth and consequent changes in telephone use. The capacity of the industry was strained, and the quality of service deteriorated. This decline triggered two regulatory responses. The Federal Communications Commission required the Bell System to compile data on nineteen service quality measurements for twenty metropolitan areas beginning in 1968; the report was subsequently expanded to cover all major Bell operating companies, and the number of indexes was reduced to ten. Less directly, the reports and the service quality issue surfaced in the federal and state commissions so that American Telephone and Telegraph (AT&T) was motivated to embark on a major investment program (without apparent expectations of substantial additional profit from the program). The resulting new capital stock improved productivity, reduced the vulnerability of the telephone companies to changes in wage rates and to job actions, and helped improve service quality from the depressed levels of the late 1960s. The service quality changes in the telephone industry over the last ten years are shown in table 26.

Airline service quality fell in the 1970s as the carriers limited their acquisitions of new equipment, reduced flight frequencies by

TABLE 26

SERVICE QUALITY IN THE TELEPHONE INDUSTRY, 1969–1978
(1969 = 100)

Service Quality Measurement	1973	1978
Toll and assistance answer delay	87	95
Installation appointments not met	187	314
Unfilled regrades	108	212
Trunk blockages and failures	147	250
Dial tone delay	216	325

NOTE: Higher index indicates improved service.
SOURCE: American Telephone and Telegraph, *Quality of Service, 75–Area Report* (1979).

TABLE 27

SERVICE QUALITY IN THE AIRLINE INDUSTRY, 1965–1978
(base year = 100)

Index (Base Year)	1965	1969	1973	1978
Q.S.I. (1961)	137	201	199	163
Load factor (1958)	109	119	116	106
Seating density (1973)	n.a.	n.a.	100	95

n.a. = not available.
NOTE: Higher index indicates improved service.
SOURCES: See table 7 for Q.S.I. and load-factor indexes. Seating-density data are authors' calculations based on Civil Aeronautics Board, *Air Carrier Operating Cost and Performance Report* (1974, 1979); see also table 31 below.

retiring smaller aircraft in favor of the stretched and wide-body models, and improved equipment utilization through higher seating densities. These changes are evident from the systematic declines of the quality indexes during the mid-1970s (see table 27).

Railroad service quality continued to decline. During the 1970s, however, an increasing proportion of railroad freight traffic began to move outside the regulated rate structure. Greater use of customer-specific rolling stock and implicit contracting between shipper and carrier provided a quality of service superior to the standard carload service. Although neither the specialized nor the standard services necessarily improved during this period, the shift in traffic mix to the better service makes the aggregated quality indexes somewhat ambiguous (see table 28). Thus, the loss-and-damage performance of the rails recovered from earlier declines. But the more de-

TABLE 28

SERVICE QUALITY IN THE RAILROAD INDUSTRY, 1965–1978
(1958 = 100)

Index	1965	1969	1973	Latest Year
Loss and damage[a]	89	73	90	109 (1977)
Turnaround time				
Boxcars	100	90	88	73 (1977)
All cars	113	112	111	95 (1977)
Percentage of cars serviceable				
Boxcars	92	100	99	93 (1978)
All other cars	103	104	104	102 (1978)

NOTE: Higher index indicates improved service.
[a] Base year 1960 = 100.
SOURCES: For loss and damage and turnaround time, see table 7; for serviceable cars, see Interstate Commerce Commission, *Annual Report* (various years).

tailed measures show the extent of deterioration. Boxcar turnaround time worsened by some 20 percent over the 1969–1977 period. This may be contrasted with the more stable average for all cars, which includes those in specialized service. Also, the serviceability of boxcars declined both in absolute terms and in relation to the average for other car types.

With little new equipment being added to systems, the air and rail carriers were offering less frequency, comfort, or convenience to passengers or shippers. As profit margins were falling under inflation and lagging regulation, firms were not gaining from this reduction in service. At best, they were able to mitigate the effects of narrowed margins.

The various measures of service quality indicate that the regulated companies were no longer providing significant improvements in the volume and quality of service each year. So far, these results represent only delay, inconvenience, and some loss of efficiency. But the occurrence of worsening economic conditions, or of more adverse regulatory decisions, could have further implications for service that would not be so easily accommodated. Without capacity to offer expanded or even adequate service, the companies and consumers could be faced with serious service disruptions and shortages.

4

Prospects for Improved Service

Concern with regulation and industry performance has developed among both consumer groups and regulated companies. The growth of "social regulation"—health, safety, and environmental controls—and the extension of economic regulation to new sectors such as crude oil have provoked a wide-ranging debate. Industries regulated by the traditional agencies have reacted against the way in which the controls have operated since the late 1960s. Public interest organizations have become more critical of the decline in service quality generally, and of the way in which agencies have abandoned their role of protecting and enhancing service provided to low-income and rural consumers in particular. The various parties have been dealing with different sides of the same coin: Regulation under the economic conditions of the time did not allow price levels sufficient to improve the quality and quantity of public utility and transportation services.

The widespread and adverse nature of these results generated support for revising the most severely constraining controls to achieve both more industry revenue and more service. Making such changes in regulations, however, has been difficult. Amending the control process has both short- and long-term effects that go beyond merely correcting prices and output to deal with current service problems. Even a partial lifting of controls could result in disruptive short-term price increases and changes in service offerings, particularly where there are shortages. These effects could be offset by long-term gains, but highly visible disruptions would occur immediately and the full benefits of small increases in offerings would not be realized for many years. Furthermore, partial decontrol of prices and service offerings, in which only some of the regulated markets were freed of controls, could leave the company with requirements to provide nonremunerative service in the remaining regulated markets while not being able to obtain higher than competitive profits on the decontrolled services.

Even so, the condition of the regulated industries that developed in the 1970s has made change imperative. Poor performance has not resulted from chance or even from regulatory intent, but rather has followed necessarily from the malfunctioning regulatory process. When the economy is subject to both high inflation and low economic growth, the regulatory rate-setting process has results adverse to both regulated companies and consumers. Prices must be able to respond to changes in cost and demand conditions quickly and fully, but rates cannot do so if they depend only on book costs and on averaging of these costs in some previous period. Given the poor performance in the last decade, short-term adjustment problems would seem a reasonable trade-off for the long-term gains that would ensue from allowing flexible and responsive pricing.

The potential for improvement has begun to be recognized, and some changes are now appearing. More responsive pricing systems have been tried in particular industries, and their performance has been enhanced. The success of regulatory reform in these sectors and the ability to extend similar improvements to other industries will determine the quality and quantity of regulated services over the coming decade.

The Content of Regulatory Reform

Improving rate regulation requires a process change that permits revenue increases sufficient to cover current and near-future cost increases. The existing rate case practice could be modified in several ways so that costs and revenues are accounted for contemporaneously. Future costs and revenues could be estimated and rates set to equate these values, with any resulting error in rates subject to adjustment after historical costs and revenues are subsequently determined. The practical procedure would be to allow a proposed rate increase to go into effect, if justified by acceptable forecasts, with later repayment to consumers of any realized excess profits. Excess profits would be defined as the difference between forecast (acceptable) and realized net revenues in the period during which the increased revenues were collected. Such a regulatory practice, comparing the same year's costs and prices, would be based even more securely on accounting data than the present method of comparing past costs and future prices.[1]

[1] The "future test year" procedure for estimating costs in New York Public Service Commission procedures is of this nature.

On the other hand, forward-looking rates would require the regulatory agency to substitute judgment for accounting data at the initial rate setting. If intervenors were able to extend their influence to this process, an additional downward bias on these "provisional" rates would be introduced. Given sufficient outside pressure, the agency might not permit the firm subsequently to recoup an underestimate of required revenues once the actual results for the test year are known.

While such procedures have not been widely implemented, the principle at least has become well established in recent years. The statute mandates require that commissions provide the public utility with a reasonable opportunity to earn a rate of return sufficient to maintain the company's financial integrity, attract necessary capital, and compensate investors for risk.[2] To meet this requirement, commissions and agencies generally made concessions to the economic conditions of the 1970s: automatic rate increases resulting from certain known and quantifiable increases in expenses, and the use of current or future, rather than historical, costs in revenue increase requests. Automatic adjustment of rates is now permitted to electric and gas utilities in a large number of states to account for fuel cost increases. Attempts have been made to extend automatic adjustment to costs other than fuel. The practice has not been widespread, although in a few important cases costs have been indexed to the consumer or producer price index. In New Mexico, for example, the state commission has instituted an indexing plan for the Public Service Company of New Mexico. The results have been encouraging, in that the utility has been reporting both higher profits and smaller rate increases than the national average.[3] More recently, the Michigan Public Service Commission has adopted an indexing system for Consumers Power and Detroit Edison Companies that allows pass-through of nonpower operating costs based entirely on changes in the consumer price index. These provisions, however, currently apply in only two states and would have to be adopted much more

[2] See *Bluefield Water Works & Improvement Co.* v. *Public Service Commission of the State of West Virginia*, 262 U.S. 79 (1923), pp. 692–93; *Federal Power Commission* v. *Hope Natural Gas Co.*, 320 U.S. 591 (1944), p. 603 (a regulated utility should be permitted to earn at a rate equal to that experienced by firms in industries characterized by comparable or corresponding risks).
[3] Public Service Commission of New Mexico, Case No. 1196 (April 15, 1975). In part, these results flow from the higher bond rating the utility has earned because of increased investor certainty over the adequacy of future rate increases. The utility has realized substantial savings in interest payments.

widely before the performance of the regulated industries would be significantly affected.[4]

Further, the state commissions—faced with declining service quality and more frequent rate cases—have begun to show a willingness to consider estimates of future operating costs in evaluating proposals for revenue increases. Since 1977, the New York Public Service Commission has dealt with estimates of costs in future test years, even though they have necessarily been speculative and subject to substantial errors of forecast.[5] Also, the state regulatory commissions have been hearing requests for rate increases in new procedures that have greatly reduced the time required to approve a price change. This has been done by allowing the proposed higher rates to take effect before the decision, subject to repayment of any excess charges after the decision is reached. For example, although electricity case decisions in 1977 took four months longer than in 1971, rate increases took less time to be put into effect.[6]

Most important, the regulatory agencies have been allowing larger increases. This tendency to acquiesce to higher revenue requests has resulted partly from higher estimates of costs, now that historical costs reflect the sharp increases in construction and interest expenses of the early and middle 1970s. As shown in table 29, allowed rates of return were almost two percentage points higher in 1978 than in 1973, with about the same current costs, but higher historical costs, in the later year.

The standards for deciding what are to be included in costs have also been changed significantly, thus permitting larger revenue increases. The revisions have varied from state to state, of course, but most commissions in recent years have permitted the inclusion of expenditures on construction work in progress (CWIP) in capital costs for rate-making purposes. With quite substantial construction projects under way at the time of the change, particularly in the electric power industry, this practice substantially increased the possibility of justifying revenue increases. Also, some states have changed their treatment of the federal tax savings from accelerated depreciation and the investment tax credit to allow the utilities to

[4] Passthrough of costs for some inputs but not others could introduce a bias toward selecting technologies relatively intensive in those inputs for which cost recovery is assured. Provisions for automatic fuel adjustment only, for example, could discourage the shift away from fuel-intensive processes.
[5] Michela English, "The Problem of Attracting Capital Faced by Investor-Owned Electric Utilities and Possible Regulatory Solutions," Working Paper Series A, No. 38, Yale University, School of Organization and Management (1979), p. 28.
[6] Edison Electric Institute, *1978 Annual Electric Power Survey* (1978).

TABLE 29

RETURNS ALLOWED TO THE ELECTRIC UTILITIES, 1971–1978

Year	Number of Cases	Total Sales Revenue in Test Year (billions of dollars)	Total Increased Sales Revenue Sought (billions of dollars)	Average Rate of Return Sought (percent)	Average Rate of Return Granted (percent)	Amount Granted as a Percent of Amount Sought
1971	59	11.3	0.9	7.61	7.44	72.7
1972	101	9.6	1.0	8.01	7.64	65.6
1973	86	11.2	1.2	7.59	7.50	74.9
1974	96	12.9	1.9	8.60	8.27	79.8
1975	118	19.9	3.6	9.08	8.60	69.6
1976	131	25.3	4.5	8.35	7.88	49.0
1977	128	26.3	3.5	9.67	9.07	55.1
1978[a]	32	3.6	0.5	9.69	9.09	63.1

[a] Incomplete.
SOURCE: Compiled from data on individual companies as reported by Edison Electric Institute.

retain more of the net cash flow from these provisions. The coverage of these changes in state regulatory practice is given in table 30; their effect on earnings and investment has yet to be determined.

Considerable reform of telephone regulation occurred in the last few years following state and federal decisions on competitive entry in markets served by the large common carrier. With markets opened for long-distance private-line business communications, the profit margins on that service have declined. Lacking funding for cross-subsidization from these interstate services, the regulatory agencies no longer look to the Bell System and the large independent telephone companies to "rate average" to hold down residential charges. As a result, the rate structure has become much more cost-oriented.[7] While basic residential monthly charges remain low, the "unbundling" of services has resulted in sharply higher service connection charges for business users and more usage-sensitive charges for both businesses and residences.[8]

[7] As of July 1979, multi-element service connection charges (six elements) were in effect in forty-six jurisdictions; American Telephone and Telegraph, 1979.
[8] See Bell Telephone Laboratories, Inc., *Engineering and Operations in the Bell System* (Murray Hill, N.J.: 1977), pp. 72–82.

TABLE 30

ADMINISTRATIVE REFORMS IN ELECTRIC UTILITY REGULATION,
1978–1979

(number of states permitting use of reform)

Reform[a]	Full Use	Partial Use	No Use
Future test year	12	6	32
Automatic fuel adjustment clause	43	—	7
Construction work in progress (CWIP)	22	17	11
Normalized tax savings	40	5	5

NOTE: All tabulations include the District of Columbia and exclude Nebraska, which has no investor-owned electric utilities.
[a] These reforms are explained in the text.
SOURCES: Merrill Lynch, Pierce, Fenner & Smith, Inc., Securities Research Division, "Utility Research: Recent Regulatory Decisions and Trends" (January 1979); Edison Electric Institute, "Survey on Construction Work in Progress in Rate Base" (October 1978).

These changes in regulatory practice have been, for the most part, in the right direction, but they have not gone far enough to reverse the widespread decline in the services provided by these industries. More drastic reforms are in process, including complete elimination of regulation in the transportation industries and restructuring of markets for electric, gas, and telephone services. These proposals have some promise, particularly in light of the limited procedural reform to date; so they deserve closer examination.

Deregulation and Other Major Reforms

The potential for reform can be seen in the results from the limited deregulation that has taken place so far in some regulated industries. The most widely publicized forays into deregulation have occurred in the airline and gas industries. These cases can be considered representative of the issues and prospects.

Until recently, the domestic passenger airlines had been operating under stringent price and market entry controls, and consequently were having difficulty making a reasonable profit within the rate structure allowed by the Civil Aeronautics Board. After controls were loosened by the CAB in the mid-1970s, Congress amended major sections of the Federal Aviation Act so that entry and price controls could be lifted over a period of years. The CAB supported this repeal. Chairman John Robson stated the agency's view in this period: "Because of [regulatory] inefficiencies, neither the airlines nor the consumer has fully reaped the potential benefit of the industry's enormous past productivity gains and growth."[9] With the enactment of the Airline Deregulation Act of 1978, traffic increased sharply as discount fares filled off-peak capacity. At the same time, standard coach fares increased within the CAB transition guidelines sufficiently to make up for most cost changes into 1979 (see table 31). But controls were still sufficiently binding to cause partially regulated fares to fall behind fuel cost increases starting in late 1979.[10] Traffic and service have grown apace, so that realized levels of service quality are no higher today than they were on the eve of deregulation. Such growth has occasionally exceeded the physical capacity of the industry, however, particularly in airport facilities and aircraft. In some instances, deregulation has meant reduced service. With small communities protected from service interruptions by provisions of the deregulation legislation, negative consequences have appeared in those cities—Bakersfield, California, and Columbus, Georgia, for example—whose "intermediate" size made them especially vulnerable to the perturbations of the free market. Several such cities have lost most or all trunk service. While replacement service by commuter air carriers was eventually established, transition problems arose in few cases causing some disruption and in some instances further deterioration. In Columbus, for example, departures were down 23 percent and seats 46 percent for the year ending June 30, 1979.[11] Moreover, air travelers often consider the service in the smaller turboprop aircraft flown by commuter carriers to be inferior to that previously provided by the larger carriers in jets, even if scheduling and seat availability have improved.

Natural gas prices were substantially decontrolled in 1975–1979. Significant shortages had occurred in the early and middle 1970s, and the curtailments regulatory system had shifted them almost entirely to the interstate markets, as producers sold uncommitted production in unregulated intrastate markets at higher than regulated prices (see table 32). Congress attempted to restructure these markets and reform regulation in the Natural Gas Policy Act of 1978 (NGPA) by forcing gas from unregulated intrastate markets into

[9] U.S. Congress, House of Representatives, Subcommittee on Aviation of the Committee on Public Works, *Hearings on Aviation Regulatory Reform*, 95th Congress, 1st session, April 18, 1977.
[10] Authors' calculations based on Civil Aeronautics Board, *Air Carrier Financial Statistics* (various issues, 1979).
[11] Civil Aeronautics Board, *Report on Airline Service* (various issues).

TABLE 31

Results of Airline Regulatory Reform, 1973–1980

	Measures of Output and Price (average annual rates of change, in percent)			
	1973–1977	1977–1978	1978–1979	1979–1980[a]
Revenue passenger-miles	5.4	16.7	11.1	1.5
Average fare yield	6.5	−1.6	5.7	16.5
Standard coach fare	7.3	7.2	14.4	20.0

	Measures of Service Quality (1973 = 100)			
	1977	1978	1979	1980[a]
Q.S.I.[b]	80	82	86	78
Load factor	93	85	82	92
Seating density[c]	98	95	93	<93

n.a. = not available.

Note: Results are for all domestic trunk and local service carriers.

[a] Estimated from partial data.

[b] Q.S.I. = quality of service index.

[c] Unweighted average for domestic trunk carriers' B727–100/200, B747, and L–1011 aircraft.

Sources: Civil Aeronautics Board, *Air Carrier Traffic Statistics* (various issues), *Air Carrier Financial Statistics* (various issues), *Aircraft Operating Cost and Performance Report* (various issues), and "Seasonally Adjusted Capacity and Traffic" (December 1979); see also table 7.

interstate markets. The NGPA used an incremental pricing system to effect phased decontrol of natural gas markets. In the first of two phases, the incremental system held residential prices below equilibrium, shifting the shortage to industrial users and squeezing the shortage out entirely by passing through large wellhead price increases to industrial users. In this way, the NGPA sought to institutionalize the subsidization practiced in these industries during the previous decade.[12] By the end of 1979, the controlled price of gas, though higher than the year before, had fallen even further behind the world unregulated price.[13] The introduction of numerous bills

[12] Paul W. MacAvoy, "The Natural Gas Policy Act of 1978," *Natural Resources Journal*, vol. 19 (October 1979), pp. 811–28.

[13] U.S. Department of Energy, "Financial Statistics of Electrical Utilities and Interstate Natural Gas Pipeline Companies," Energy Data Report (December 1979), table 4. Domestic prices at wholesale went from $0.96 per thousand cubic feet (MCF) to $1.35, while the price of imports increased from $2.15 per MCF to $3.54.

TABLE 32

PRICES AND QUANTITIES FOR NATURAL GAS, 1965–1979
(average annual rates of change, in percent)

Years	Interstate Regulated Sales		Intrastate Unregulated Sales		Imported Sales	
	Price	Quantity	Price	Quantity	Price	Quantity
1965–1969	1.21	7.48	2.81	1.28	0.37	14.35
1969–1972	5.61	1.50	19.37	5.18	7.80	13.61
1972–1977	27.51	−4.78	41.99	−15.05	45.26	0.38
1977–1979	20.34	3.05	—[a]	−4.63[a]	14.33	10.79

[a] Intrastate sales regulated by Federal Energy Regulatory Commission under the Natural Gas Policy Act of 1978.
SOURCES: Federal Power Commission, *Sales by Producers of Natural Gas to Interstate Pipeline Companies, 1972* (June 1974); U.S. Department of Energy, Energy Information Administration, *Energy Data Reports: Interstate Gas Prices and Financial Data* (March 1978) Federal Power Commission and Federal Energy Regulatory Commission, biannual and quarterly news releases on intrastate natural gas prices (1957–1977); and Department of Energy, *Monthly Energy Review* (May 1980).

in Congress in response to the rise in unregulated prices makes eventual decontrol appear less than certain. Whether complete deregulation is ultimately achieved will depend on whether there are enough field and supplemental supplies under the second phase to meet all industrial gas demands at the higher schedule of prices.

Deregulation has proceeded at a slower pace in the other regulated industries. One example is railroads, the first of these industries to be regulated. The Railroad Revitalization and Regulatory Reform Act of 1975 (the 4R Act) provided for deregulation in those markets where railroads did not dominate "transportation services" and where adjustment of rates by the companies themselves would allow them to meet competitive conditions. Both the 4R Act and the Interstate Commerce Commission defined "dominance" so broadly, however, that rate decontrol occurred in only a few markets; it was not until 1979–1980, with a revitalized commission, that more than half of freight tonnage moved under deregulated rate schedules.[14]

---

[14] Section 202 of the 4R Act, amending Sections 1(5) and 15 of the Interstate Commerce Act, was intended to remove ICC maximum rate regulation authority in situations where railroads faced effective competition but to retain it in situations of rail "market dominance." In implementing Section 202, the ICC developed presumptive rules under which market dominance would be found to exist. In a court challenge, the ICC regulations were upheld in a decision based almost entirely on deference to the ICC's presumed expertise. See *Atchison, Topeka and Santa Fe Railway Co.* v. *ICC and*

The Railroad Deregulation Act of 1979 would have substantially reduced regulation of the railroads further, if its proposed changes in rate regulation, abandonment procedures, and merger rules had gone into effect. After a five-year transition period, there would have been no maximum or minimum rate regulation; rather, charges for railroad services would have been set by market forces where the railroads competed with other forms of transportation. Abandonment would have been simplified by requiring a railroad line to meet only the most rudimentary conditions for termination in order to gain approval. Mergers would no longer have been reviewed by the Interstate Commerce Commission, but would have been subject only to the general antitrust provisions governing all industry. This proposed legislation addressed the issues that were causing the major problems for the railroads. Congress eventually approved much less sweeping legislation that falls short of deregulation. The amendments will loosen some price controls and relax conditions for rail line abandonment. The ICC will continue to enforce rate ceilings and service requirements on standard carload services, however, even beyond the end of the transition period in 1984. Whether this increased pricing freedom leads to improved service quality thus still depends on the reaction of the regulatory agency to increases in company costs.

In the telephone industry, progress on regulatory reform was evident in 1980. Congress debated legislation to permit increased competition in long-distance service, terminal equipment, and data processing applications. The proposals would permit new firms to enter the Bell System's previously closed long-distance markets, require universal access to the local switching facilities, and relax some of the restrictions on Bell's entry into nontelephone fields. A schedule of access charges and surcharges on long-distance usage would be implemented to defray some of the costs for the local and rural telephone services currently supported by internal subsidies. Opposition to the legislation came from the smaller independent tele-

---

United States, 580 F.2d 623 (D.C. Cir. 1978). The regulations have been criticized as being overrestrictive, however, since they neglect actual competition from other modes, if it cannot be measured adequately, and since they ignore potential competition entirely. See U.S. Department of Transportation, *Report on the Regulatory Reform Provisions of the Railroad Revitalization and Regulatory Reform Act of 1976* (February 1976), p. 22. A study commissioned by the ICC estimated that 48.5 percent of total rail traffic would trigger at least one presumptive test. See Interstate Commerce Commission, *The Impact of the 4–R Railroad Ratemaking Provisions* (October 5, 1977), pp. 8–9. Because of the restrictive nature of the presumptive rules, the ICC in effect has frustrated any rate flexibility that the railroads thought they had obtained in the legislation. See Paul W. MacAvoy, ed., *Unsettled Questions on Regulatory Reform* (Washington, D.C.: American Enterprise Institute, 1978), p. 20.

phone companies, who feared reduced subsidization of their operations, and from some public interest groups wary of the antitrust implications of permitting AT&T to enter new markets.

By 1980, the deregulation movement could claim some modest gains. Certainly airlines had become more competitive and more productive, with profits initially well above earlier (1975) levels. From the perspective of the consumer, however, performance was more mixed. Average fares, which fell initially under deregulation, were boosted sharply by escalating fuel prices. Deep discount fares on some high-density routes were coupled with higher base fares and reduced service quality in some markets. In addition, profits have shrunk drastically with the onset of the recession.

The other activities undertaken in the name of deregulation have come to little more than an institutionalization of the adjustment to cost inflation. The Natural Gas Policy Act, assuming Congress permits the decontrol process to reach its conclusion, may bring forth sufficient new gas to forestall further service curtailments. But this depends on the willingness of industrial users to increase their subsidies so that service to residential consumers can be expanded and improved. The 4R Act, as practiced under judicial interpretation, has been seen as a partial solution to the basic regulatory problems of the railroads.

Also, the proponents of reform must begin to consider explicitly the problems involved in making the transition to a less-regulated environment. The phased deregulation of airlines and natural gas companies was the result of political compromises over the timing of income redistributions rather than an effort to promote efficiency during and after the adjustment period; important efficiency considerations remain to be addressed. The fears of a destabilizing dynamic process leading to "competitive chaos" and widespread disruption have not been realized. Lesser problems of speculative purchasing, production inefficiency, scattered service interruptions, and adverse market structure developments, however, have been observed in both the airline and the natural gas cases. It remains to be seen whether any campaign to reduce controls can overcome short-term problems and lead to improvements in service in these industries.

The Outlook for Service in the Regulated Industries

Regulation under economic conditions like those of the 1970s reduces the growth and quality of service in the controlled sector of the economy. Service has been reduced in almost all cases, as the companies have reacted to narrowed rate-cost margins by cutting back growth. The special considerations for home and rural consumers in electricity, natural gas, and telephone have all but disappeared, because these industries have not made the capital investments necessary to maintain and expand production. Reduced investment and consequent service quality reductions were noted first in the late 1960s in the natural gas and telephone industries. The same service deterioration would have appeared in electric power by the late 1970s, except for unexpected reduced demand growth resulting from the 1973–1974 energy crisis and economy-wide fuel inflation.

In these and the other regulated industries, the outlook for consumers remains cloudy with respect to both quality and the coverage of service. As shown in table 33, each of the regulated industries will require extremely large investments to maintain the same level of service in the 1980s as in the late 1970s. The outlook for obtaining these amounts from internal financing and the capital markets depends crucially on the regulatory environment. A continuation of pre-existing regulations generally would cause capital shortfalls, which would lead to continued deterioration in service in these industries. Fulfilling the promises of regulatory reform, on the other hand, would imply at least the maintenance of current service levels.

The telephone companies appear to be able to meet all of their external financing requirements, given that there may be somewhat more limited service growth. Industry profitability may be reduced in high-margin markets as traffic is diverted to independent and unregulated microwave transmission companies specializing in business services. But profitability will not likely increase in low-margin markets because of commission resistance to sharp increases in basic service rates. Absent such rate relief, the Bell System and other companies would then experience an overall decline in profitability, which must lead to reduced investment and ultimately reduced service. This may take a number of years, however, as productivity gains in the near future continue to moderate cost increases.

The outlook for the transportation and energy companies is less promising. For the airlines, projections of aircraft replacement and expansion demands, and comparison with the levels of cash flow required to finance such equipment, indicate an inability under continued partial regulation to finance a substantial expansion of air passenger service. The Air Transport Association has predicted $90 billion in capital investments by the industry during the 1980s under relatively optimistic assumptions.[15] Fleet additions requiring roughly

[15] Air Transport Association, "$90 Billion by '90: Airline Capital Investment in the 1980's" (September 1979).

TABLE 33

THE OUTLOOK FOR CAPACITY
IN THE REGULATED INDUSTRIES IN THE 1980s
(billions of current dollars)

Industry	Capital Requirements	Required External Financing	Notional Potential Shortfall
Electric	540–621	325–398	275
Natural gas	75	n.a.	13
Telephone	89–116	18–23	0
Airline	34	10–13	0–7
Railroad	43–55	5–33	5–16

n.a. = not available.

SOURCES: Data are ranges based on various capital outlook studies and authors' estimates.

Electric: David L. Scott, "Financing the Growth of Electric Utilities" (New York, 1976); Federal Power Commission, *The Financial Outlook for the Electric Power Industry*, National Power Survey Advisory Committee Report (1974); Martin Baughman and Dilip P. Damat, "Financing the Future Growth of the Electric Power Industry" (University of Texas at Austin, September 1978).

Natural gas: American Gas Association, "A Forecast of the Economic Demand for Gas Energy in the U.S. through 1990" (February 9, 1979) and "A Forecast of Capital Requirements of the U.S. Gas Utility Industry to the Year 2000" (April 20, 1979).

Telephone: Paine, Weber, Jackson, and Curtis Inc. (1976); Goldman, Sachs Inc., unpublished estimates (May 1979).

Airline: Donaldson, Lufkin, and Jenerette, *Domestic Truck Airlines: The Coming Era of Capital-Constrained Prosperity* (December 1978).

Railroad: U.S. Department of Transportation, *A Prospectus for Change in the Freight Railroad Industry: A Preliminary Report by the Secretary of Transportation* (October 1978); First National City Bank, "A Capital Market's Analysis of the Final System Plan as Proposed by the United States Railway Association" (September 1975); U.S. Congress, Office of Technology Assessment, *A Review of National Railroad Issues*, prepared at the request of the U.S. Senate, Committee on Commerce, by Harbridge House, Inc. (1975); Interstate Commerce Commission, Ex Parte No. 271 (1976).

$34 billion in capital expenditures are projected as necessary to achieve a 7 percent annual growth in traffic by 1985 even at high load factors and seating densities. Two-thirds of that amount would likely be forthcoming from depreciation and profit returns assuming a continuation of the present transition to deregulation. Even though deregulation appears to have improved the ability of the airlines to finance new investment, a comparison of airline demand projections with cash flow requirements indicates an inability under continued partial regulation to accommodate a substantial expansion of service. Air fares have already risen sharply, but still not enough to compensate fully for escalating fuel prices. Moreover, with an important new proposed noise abatement rule for older aircraft and continued fuel price inflation hastening the retirement or reengining of this equipment, the quantity of remaining capacity will be reduced and replacement or expansion costs increased. The CAB moved in 1980 to remedy this situation by lifting the ceiling on airline fares; congressional opposition and a public interest group's lawsuit, however, threaten to limit the rate flexibility to follow from this measure. If partial controls persist into the mid-1980s, aircraft seating will likely be both less plentiful and less spacious.

The outlook for the natural gas industry depends on the manner in which the Natural Gas Policy Act is implemented. Under any plausible course of events, however, shortages will continue to exist through the mid-1980s, even assuming that the maximum technically feasible level of exploration and development is undertaken by the gas and oil companies in response to higher, partially decontrolled field prices. But new production may fall short of the maximum feasible, given the mandated transition price schedule, as additional billions of dollars not forthcoming from cash flow or financing would be required to achieve these production levels between 1980 and 1985 (see table 33). The problem here is a lack of external financing and the uncertainty over future prices. Curtailments will undoubtedly continue, and consumption of substitute fuels will be increased.

Capacity shortages loom for the electric power industry. The ability to expand supply has increased somewhat as regulation has become less stringent, and could still be sufficient to meet expected consumer demands until the late 1980s. Too, the continuing pass-through of higher fuel costs has held demand growth below expectations. But in holding allowed returns on equity to less than 12 percent in the face of interest rates at higher levels, the regulatory commissions are precipitating financial difficulties and associated capital shortages in the electric power industry. Because of these supply constraints and reduced demand estimates, planned generating facilities totaling 62,829 megawatts capability were canceled between 1974 and 1978.[16] This represents approximately 12 percent of total U.S. generating capacity in 1978.[17] By the later 1980s, these conditions could result in power curtailments as lower prices create greater growth in demand and reduced growth in capacity. The Western Systems Coordinating Council, whose member utilities had an average reserve margin of 37.8 percent against the 1978 summer peak load, has nevertheless predicted imminent shortages for the

[16] Edison Electric Institute, *Electric Power Survey* (various years).
[17] Edison Electric Institute, *1979 Annual Electric Power Survey* (April 1979), p. 6.

Northwest Power Pool and the Rocky Mountain Power Area.[18] The Puget Sound Power & Light Co. has received permission from the Washington State Utilities and Transportation Commission to deny service to new residential customers for space heating and hot water.[19] Of course, the return required to prevent such shortages varies from one company to another, depending on rates of growth in consumption and operating expenses in that company's jurisdiction. But it is estimated that allowed equity returns would have to be at least four points above the prime interest rate to attract sufficient financing, even under the "easy money" market conditions of the middle 1970s.

Allowed returns, as set by the commissions, have not been high enough to provide the capital funds necessary to build capacity to prevent power shortages in the late 1980s. Financing and therefore investment are forecast to fall short of requirements by 45 percent (see table 33). Some rate relief will be forthcoming, of course, and utilities may find ways of slowing the growth in peak demand. Periodic outages, however, will likely still occur by the end of the decade, and they could lead to mandated curtailments of "nonessential uses" of electricity.[20]

Thus, the outlook for these industries is uncertain. With continued difficulty in adjusting regulated rates to changing demands and costs, there would be disinvestment by deferral of maintenance and by service abandonments. Even with reductions in service and with some rate relief, a shortfall of total capital requirements is likely.

[18] Western Systems Coordinating Council, "Coordinated Bulk Power Supply Program, 1979–1989" (1979), pp. 3B–8, 3B–9: "[T]here is a probability that the resources devoted in the Western Portion of the pool . . . will be insufficient to meet the total energy load, under adverse hydro conditions, in the 1980–84 period ranging from 36 percent in 1980–81 to 66 percent in 1983–84. Small deficiencies appear under median hydro conditions in 1984. . . . Delays in unit installations have produced only small peak demand deficiencies to date; however, peak demand reserve margins are projected to decrease and energy deficits . . . are projected to increase significantly with each additional delay." National Electric Reliability Council, "Assessment of the Overall Adequacy of the Bulk Power Supply Systems in the Electric Utility Industry of North America, Summer of 1980" (May 15, 1980), pp. 8–9: "This summer it is expected that the transmission system within the Rocky Mountain Power Area will be loaded beyond the 'withstand limits' for single contingency outages, such as the loss of a generating unit or major transmission line. As a result, generation reserves and transmission support may not be available to prevent shedding of firm load should such emergencies arise."
[19] "Power Companies That Refuse to Connect," Business Week (September 1, 1980), pp. 25–26.
[20] At the same time, utilities may be forced to invest in less capital-intensive technologies to reduce financing needs and construction time, but at higher fuel costs and lower productivity growth. Because fuel costs can be passed through to consumers more easily than capital costs, this may be the politically acceptable alternative in some cases.

This capital shortage will manifest itself in curtailments or reduced quality of product or service at fixed rates.

Such is the prognosis if the economy continues to operate with regulation much as it now occurs. A more favorable scenario is possible. Those industries in which regulation is changed slightly will perform somewhat better, with fewer shortages or disruptions of service. But great difficulties continue to block those substantial reforms required to produce significant improvements in industry performance. An unfortunate characteristic of regulation in these industries has been that the consequences of current policies are unplanned, untimely, undesirable, and yet resistant to change.

Index

Selected AEI Publications

Regulation: The AEI Journal on Government and Society, published bi-monthly (one year, $12; two years, $22; single copy, $2.50)

A Conversation with Alfred E. Kahn (26 pp., $3.25)

Reforming Regulation, Timothy B. Clark, Marvin H. Kosters, and James C. Miller III, eds. (162 pp., paper $6.25, cloth $14.25)

A Conversation with Douglas Costle (24 pp., $2.25)

Perspectives on Postal Service Issues, Roger Sherman, ed. (228 pp., paper $7.25, cloth $10.25)

A Conversation with Commissioner Eleanor Holmes Norton (23 pp., $2.25)

Vehicle Safety Inspection Systems: How Effective? W. Mark Crain (70 pp., $4.25)

U.S. Industry in Trouble: What Is the Government's Responsibility? Peter Hackes, mod. (18 pp., $3.75)

Regulatory Reform in Air Cargo Transportation, Lucile Sheppard Keyes (56 pp., $4.25)

Prices subject to change without notice.

AEI Associates Program

The American Enterprise Institute invites your participation in the competition of ideas through its AEI Associates Program. This program has two objectives:

The first is to broaden the distribution of AEI studies, conferences, forums, and reviews, and thereby to extend public familiarity with the issues. AEI Associates receive regular information on AEI research and programs, and they can order publications and cassettes at a savings.

The second objective is to increase the research activity of the American Enterprise Institute and the dissemination of its published materials to policy makers, the academic community, journalists, and others who help shape public attitudes. Your contribution, which in most cases is partly tax deductible, will help ensure that decision makers have the benefit of scholarly research on the practical options to be considered before programs are formulated. The issues studied by AEI include:

- Defense Policy
- Economic Policy
- Energy Policy
- Foreign Policy
- Government Regulation
- Health Policy
- Legal Policy
- Political and Social Processes
- Social Security and Retirement Policy
- Tax Policy

For more information, write to:

AMERICAN ENTERPRISE INSTITUTE
1150 Seventeenth Street, N.W.
Washington, D.C. 20036